Treble Triumph

Treble
Triumph

MY INSIDE STORY OF
MANCHESTER CITY'S
GREATEST-EVER SEASON

Vincent Kompany

with Ian Cheeseman

**SIMON &
SCHUSTER**

London · New York · Sydney · Toronto · New Delhi

A CBS COMPANY

First published in Great Britain by Simon & Schuster UK Ltd, 2019
A CBS COMPANY

1 3 5 7 9 10 8 6 4 2

Simon & Schuster UK Ltd
1st Floor
222 Gray's Inn Road
London WC1X 8HB

www.simonandschuster.co.uk
www.simonandschuster.com.au
www.simonandschuster.co.in

Simon & Schuster Australia, Sydney
Simon & Schuster India, New Delhi

Photography in plate sections © Getty Images

A CIP catalogue record for this book is available from the British Library

Hardback ISBN: 978-1-4711-9017-9
eBook ISBN: 978-1-4711-9018-6

Typeset in Bembo by M Rules
Printed in the UK by CPI Group (UK) Ltd, Croydon, CR0 4YY

CONTENTS

FOREWORD BY KEVIN DE BRUYNE

It's fair to say that Vinny and I have a special relationship. I've played football with him for a decade now, not all at City of course. We started playing together when I was only seventeen or eighteen for the Belgian national team. I made my debut in 2010 and Vinny was already a key player for our country.

At the time, City, through Txiki Begiristain, were trying to sign me from Wolfsburg and Vinny was pushing for me to move to Manchester to play alongside him. He called me a couple of times a week during the summer when I was still in Germany, waiting to see what had happened with the transfer. He would constantly ask me when I was coming, saying 'you need to come', always encouraging me to join City.

There's no doubt that it's easier joining a club where you know someone already – they can help you settle into the area and get to know your new teammates quickly. As captain he knew everyone very well, so I was confident he would help to make the move easy, which of course he did. That type of trust helps your friendship to grow even more. It's possible that he has always felt protective towards me; he's a little older than me. But, while I appreciate it, I don't think I need to be protected, especially from any criticism I might get from the media in Belgium.

By the time we played together at City I wasn't a child any more. I think his protectiveness was more evident when we were away with the national team. There's definitely a difference in Belgium. Some of the press back home would constantly draw comparisons between me and Eden [Hazard]. That stopped about three or four years ago, but I think Vinny has been so supportive to me because of the connection we had together at City.

Vinny is a really important player for Belgium. He was one of the first to make a big transfer to another country and because he did well the Belgian market opened up. More players followed him, like Marouane Fellaini to Everton. It meant that people in other leagues started to notice footballers from our country. They realised, perhaps for the first time, that Belgians had some talent. More and more players got the opportunity to play in bigger leagues. He created a pathway for players from Belgium.

In his last season at City he played a big role in what we achieved at the club. He kept everyone on their toes. It was a very different season from the year before when we had much more breathing space. I suppose you could say the Centurions season was a little bit more relaxed, whereas during his final campaign we had to win every game from January onwards.

In those circumstances, everyone has to be fully focused and pulling in the same direction. Behind the scenes he did a lot, but it was a triumph for him and he played his role perfectly. He recognised what we all needed to do, which is one of his many strengths. It's a team game and he was always playing his part even when he wasn't in the team, but of course during the last couple of months he played in all the games. He contributed massively on the field, too.

He fulfilled his role as captain just as well during the week as when he played. Vinny is a wanderer, he's always here, there and everywhere, always moving, talking and interacting with people. I know he did lots we weren't aware of. I'm sure there were many occasions when he talked to people on our behalf, making important points, and we wouldn't even notice. He would talk to coaches and other members of staff all the time. He'd always stay behind after we'd finished training for the day.

A couple of times a year, Vinny stood up and gave speeches to us all. He did little speeches – pep talks – before games, but these were different and a bit more significant. His motivation was always to help us as a team, or to encourage individuals. No one goes through a whole season without any problems, of course.

Sometimes he wouldn't feel the need to say a lot. I think Vinny is very good at knowing what he wants to say and how to get it across. He knew exactly the points he wanted to make, so we would really listen to him. I've seen people give ten-minute speeches and towards the end no one is listening any more. Vinny might have been on his feet, addressing us, for a shorter time, but what he said was always to the point and very good.

He's intelligent and during his time as Manchester City captain I think he learned a lot, too. I suspect that during his first few years in the role he wouldn't have addressed his teammates like he did at the end of his time at City, but that's the natural growth process you get as a player and particularly as a captain.

We all know how much he is loved by the City fans. How can you not be aware of his popularity when the crowd sings, 'Here's to you, Vincent Kompany, City loves you more than you will know.' It's lovely that he gets that recognition and he fully deserves it. It's a big commitment to give nearly eleven years of your life to a team. The largest part of his career has been here at City, and to leave must be a difficult moment. I think the way his playing career ended in Manchester was beautiful.

He has a new project ahead of him now, something completely different, and I think that's why he wanted to take it. He never gave us any clues that he was planning to leave at the end of the season. I didn't think he was ready to stop playing football, but the chance to take on a new challenge at Anderlecht was just too good to miss. It was something he couldn't resist, especially as he looks to his future. Once he made that decision it all happened very quickly.

I was in the stands for that last home league game against Leicester when we had to win, feeling very nervous. It was clear that we would just need to score one goal and so I was very happy when Vinny scored. I can imagine that some people might not have wanted him to shoot when he did, but I'm glad he did. What a goal and what a relief! I've never seen him score a goal like that in training. He's never done that before, despite what he might have said afterwards.

As we walked around the pitch after the game I became aware that Vinny was crying. I'd never seen him that emotional. In his mind, I think he had already made the decision to leave City after the final game of the season, which was clearly why he was so emotional. None of us knew that at the time, but looking back at how he was and what happened that day you can understand what was going on.

Vinny was a crucial player for us during all those games

he played in towards the end of the season. He was a great leader, but it was much more than that. The way he performed showed that he can still do it at the very highest level, game after game. I think that was a huge positive for him. He didn't leave City because he had to or because he'd dropped below the level required; he just knew the time was right and that he wanted to do something different.

The treble was incredible for Vinny, for City, for the fans, for all of us. I know he had some personal problems with injuries, but the success, the trophies, what we won last season and the season before, has been amazing. When you come to City you want to win trophies, but to win six trophies in such quick succession is a lot. I have seven winners' medals now from my four years, so it means that we are doing well and hopefully it will continue. To do what we did last year should not be underestimated. It was very difficult.

Vinny is a very smart and passionate man. He's got a lot more to do and to achieve in his career. He never sits still. I hope his time at Anderlecht will be just as successful as it was at City. I've told him to keep a place in his team for me in a year or seven, when I'm finished here . . . Joking apart, I hope everything goes well for him.

He has helped me along in certain aspects of life and I learned from him without him even knowing. I think he was, and is, a very good example of how to conduct yourself as a man and a player. He does great charity work, too, which is very important to him.

As footballers, it's important to be good human beings, too, because if you're not nice, within a short space of time there will be clashes within the squad. Players like Vinny and I are judged, by the supporters and everyone else, on how we perform, but we work hard day in and day out with each other. Just like the group as a whole, we are good together and he was definitely one of the guys who set that precedent from the beginning and so it felt like everyone else had to follow.

I will definitely miss him being around City, but I'll still see him while on international duty with Belgium and I will try to watch a couple of Anderlecht's games between matches for the national team. We're still in contact, so for me it will only be a little bit different. I will see him sooner, and more often, than the other guys.

After the parade where we passed through the streets and were cheered by thousands of City supporters, Vinny made a short speech to fans. I didn't know he was going to perform his dramatic mic drop right at the end and I don't know if he planned to drop it, but Vinny does what he does, that was his moment so we just let him enjoy it. It was the perfect way for him to leave City.

INTRODUCTION

In the past, I've resisted the many offers I've had to write a book about the early part of my life and career, because I felt I'm still only young. I've seen other people bring out books relatively early in their lives and always thought that it was strange. For me, though, the time does now seem right, with my playing time at City over and having finished my career on such a high.

It also just happened to be a historic season that ended in such an emphatic and emotional way, so I see this not only as a little bit of a thank you to those who've supported me, but also as a way for me to give a bit of an insight into what it was like to be part of such an incredible team, an incredible era and what it took to get to this point. I hope that City fans, and even supporters of other clubs, will enjoy reading my account of such an extraordinary season.

At the start of the campaign I believed that the 2018–19 season would be very special, I really did. Particularly because I felt in the previous year, the Centurions season, we had been a bit unlucky, despite what we achieved, but I did think that we got better and better as the season went along. Things culminated with a record-breaking 100 points, as Gabriel Jesus scored that late goal at Southampton on the last day of the season.

This is the story of my last season at Manchester City. It finished in the most perfect way, winning every domestic competition, starting with the Community Shield in August 2018 and ending with me lifting the FA Cup at Wembley in May 2019. Along the way, I kept myself motivated during the periods when I wasn't in the team every week, and on the penultimate day of the Premier League season I scored that vital, special goal against Leicester City.

I'll talk about the friendships we've built in the team and what has made this group of players so unique. I hope you enjoy looking back on my last, amazing season as much as I have enjoyed going back through the year and remembering the special times I've enjoyed with the players, management, coaching staff and everyone at the club, especially the fans. I've been so grateful for your support; thank you from the bottom of my heart.

CHAPTER 1

AUGUST 2018

The season started for the club with a trip to the USA, but I didn't travel with the squad that represented City in the States, as I'd been playing for my country, Belgium, at the World Cup in Russia. I made the decision, along with Kevin de Bruyne, the England lads and Benjamin Mendy, to return to training in Manchester early. I think I had seven days' holiday in total after the World Cup, something like that, and we could have taken three weeks off, but we were all hungry to get back into it. There had been three games in the USA, which resulted in defeats against Borussia Dortmund and Liverpool in Chicago and New Jersey, before a win against Bayern Munich in Miami to round things off.

Pep Guardiola rang me while I was in Russia at the World Cup, in fact he rang all the players – Kevin de Bruyne, Kyle Walker, John Stones – everyone who was out there. He gave us messages of congratulations, of course. It was great to receive a call like that, but now I'm a manager I fully understand what he was thinking. I'm sure that there was a part of him that just wanted us to come back to City as early as possible, with no injury concerns, so although he wished us continued success he'll have known that getting knocked out earlier would have meant he'd have had us back preparing for the new season that bit sooner. He must have been in two minds. I have no doubt he was genuinely pleased for us, too, but clearly he wanted his squad back as soon as he could.

When he spoke to us – the others will confirm this – he asked us our thoughts on the new season with City, too, whether we wanted to come back quickly or extend our holidays. I think most of us were keen to return, but one thing we all agreed on was that we thought Kevin would benefit from a bit more of a break. Kevin agreed, and was very straightforward about it himself, telling Pep that he felt he needed longer to recover from the physical and mental fatigue he was suffering, which was completely understandable, so he didn't come back quite as soon as I did.

The rest of us wanted to come back and play in the Community Shield game, for which we knew we had to be at full strength. I felt it was important for us to win that game. It wasn't that we doubted the rest of the squad could win it without us, but we believed we would have a better chance if we were available, too.

It was a fairly young squad that had travelled to the US, though it did include our summer signing Riyad Mahrez along with Joe Hart and Oleksandr Zinchenko. The second game of the tour was at New Jersey's Met Life Stadium, by which time Bernardo Silva had joined up with the squad. The final game was against Bayern Munich in Miami, and

Bernardo was already showing signs of the form that would be so crucial to the team in the coming months by scoring twice. These were only pre-season games, but it was encouraging that the team finished off their preparations for the real games with a win and a good performance.

Although I was aware of what had happened in the games out there, to be honest I was just focusing on trying to earn a place in the starting XI for the Community Shield against Chelsea at Wembley. We all respected Maurizio Sarri, the new Chelsea manager, from his time at Napoli where they'd given us two tough games in the Champions League and so we knew it would take something special to go and beat his new team in the Community Shield.

I remember, as I returned from my mini-break, that I was really intent on observing how everyone – the players, the manager and even the fans – was going to react after winning the Premier League so convincingly the previous season. Right after winning our other league titles, I remember noticing how poorly we prepared for the following campaign. It wasn't that we as players didn't want to win any more, it's just that there seems to be something inside every human being that changes after a big success, which is understandable. The tendency is to be more relaxed. That feeling comes from knowing what you've achieved.

When you get to a certain level, you can get into a comfort zone that you don't want to be in because the other guys, your rivals and your opponents, could then want it more than you. That's not how or why we became successful in the first place.

Community Shield
Sunday 5 August
Wembley Stadium
Attendance: 72,724

MANCHESTER CITY   **2**
Aguero (13, 58)

CHELSEA   **0**

City: Claudio Bravo, Kyle Walker, John Stones, Aymeric Laporte, Benjamin Mendy, Fernandinho, Bernardo Silva, Phil Foden, Riyad Mahrez, Leroy Sane, Sergio Aguero

Subs used: Ilkay Gundogan, Gabriel Jesus, Brahim Diaz, Vincent Kompany, Nicolas Otamendi, Claudio Gomes

Unused subs: Ederson

Booked: None

I remember starting the game at Wembley on the bench and thinking, *Surely I haven't come back early and done all this to sit on the bench?* I desperately wanted to play some part in the game, but maybe I wouldn't get on the field after all. Thankfully, you're allowed more subs in the Community Shield, so I was the fourth to come on, with just ten minutes to go. I remember making one satisfying tackle and that it was a hot day, but more than anything I was pleased we got off to a winning start. As far as I was concerned, it was worth coming back off my holidays to lift silverware and, just as importantly, my wife thought the same. In the end it was the right decision, but actually it was an easy decision.

By the time I came on, we were 2–0 up and the game was won after we had completely controlled things. Any worries we'd had about Sarri's immediate impact on the side seemed to have been unnecessary, though Chelsea would go on to make a strong start to the Premier League campaign. At this stage of the season, you can't always tell much about how the rest will proceed, but this was a fine start, and I didn't have far to look for a reason.

Once we were all back together, I remember Pep Guardiola announcing a whole bunch of new rules. There were new sanctions to be introduced; there would even be fines for certain misdemeanours. We'd never had a system like that before; there had been threats of it, but it was only really for extreme cases, and then suddenly we came back at the start of the season and all these things were ready to be implemented.

For me it was interesting observing this. I think it was like a pre-emptive strike; the manager was effectively punishing the team before anything had even gone wrong, or at least that's how I saw it. Although this new system was clearly outlined by Pep, the truth is that it never needed to happen, because right from the start we just picked up where we'd left off the season before by steamrollering through the games and so he knew the lads wanted it. Pep need not have feared that the players would lack any motivation.

I came to the conclusion was that this was just an example of how desperate Pep was to win again. He's very highly motivated, as everyone knows, and he simply wanted us to be the same. His attitude made a big difference and was reflected within the team.

The hunger, the desire was evident among all the players. I could see it every day, I could see it on their faces and in everything they did. Because we had a big squad, every one of us always felt that there were younger players waiting for their chance to prove they were just as good, if not better, than we were. In reality, we were doubled up, with virtually the same level of quality and talent from two players in every position.

All the players had slight differences, of course, different profiles and attributes, and ultimately everybody would have periods in the season where they would step up and shine. You certainly couldn't point someone out in the team and say they would make us weaker at any stage. I think that was highly significant and made us more likely to be successful again, combined of course with the manager's words and coaching.

I could see that we were going to be a great team again, playing football the right way, and I believed that we would win the Premier League for a second consecutive season. But if I'm honest, I thought we'd do it by ten clear points. I never thought Liverpool would be as strong as they were.

As far as my personal physical condition was concerned, I had just come off the back of a World Cup, where we finished third, beating England in the third-place play-off, so I was feeling fine. I knew that despite Belgium's success in the World Cup I was back at City, a club with great competition for places. I think we had a healthy rivalry.

I want City to win, of course I do. Ultimately you could say that my faith in what I believe, and my career, depended on them all doing well, too – even those with whom I was competing for a place in the team. If I were to come back into a team that had been losing games, it would probably mean that we wouldn't be winning any silverware. I wished no ill on my teammates, even though I'd want to be playing at every opportunity.

The season before, we'd had a very healthy rotation between all the centre backs; we all got to play and we all had our special moments. I was really happy for this to happen. This season would prove to be slightly different because once it properly started, the manager decided to lock in the left centre back position and that made the competition so much harder for me than the season before. Aymeric Laporte is left-footed and Pep prefers to play a naturally left-sided player in that role. That meant that, in Pep's opinion, Laporte became the natural selection for almost every game and of course the manager has the right to make that decision, but it meant it often became a competition between three players for the remaining place.

It was clear that the opportunities would be a lot scarcer for me, John Stones and Nicolas Otamendi. Don't misunderstand me, I think Pep still took squad rotation into account and other things too, but that didn't help my chances of playing lots of games. He was prioritising the future by giving Stones a lot of valuable match time. I understood that. In the future I might make the same types of decisions myself, so I totally understood where I was in the grand scheme of things. Experience gives you a calmness and I have always believed in myself. I knew very well that no trophies are won in September, so I needed to be patient.

It wasn't just me either: Fernandinho and David Silva showed great examples to the rest of the squad when they weren't being picked. If the 'ex-key players' behave in the right way when they're not selected, then that gives no one else in the squad an excuse to behave any differently. It sets a benchmark.

As captain, I felt I had a particular responsibility to set a good example. Of course, every player wants to play, but the decisions Pep was making weren't just based on the quality of the individual. By the end of it, the team had become such a machine that you could never fault the manager. Every decision he made was the right one. But what it meant was that, for us three especially, we couldn't afford to put a foot wrong.

We were determined to start the season strongly. Over 72,000 fans were packed into Wembley and we were determined that there would be nothing taken for granted. This was our first chance to show everyone that we intended to start where we left off at Southampton the previous season.

For Aguero it was another day of writing himself in the history books, with his opening goal being his 200th for the club in all competitions. He took it left-footed after a great pass from Phil Foden. Forty-five minutes later, he began his search to complete a third hundred when Bernardo Silva set him up and he finished well. By contrast, Chelsea hardly managed a shot on target all game.

It was a really hot day, with water breaks during play and some of us on the bench wore wet towels on our heads to keep us cool. But no matter how much sweat and effort you have to go through, a trophy is a trophy and standing at the top of the steps and lifting some silverware, whatever it is, never gets any less exciting. Once again I had the honour of raising the Community Shield high to show it to our amazing fans. We'd got the new season off to a winning start and we had a trophy to show for our efforts. All we had to do now was keep it going once the Premier League campaign started.

Premier League (1)
Sunday 12 August
Emirates Stadium
Attendance: 59,934

ARSENAL	**0**
MANCHESTER CITY	**2**

Sterling (14), Bernardo Silva (64)

City: Ederson, Kyle Walker, John Stones, Aymeric Laporte, Benjamin Mendy, Fernandinho, Ilkay Gundogan, Riyad Mahrez, Bernardo Silva, Sergio Aguero, Raheem Sterling

Subs used: Kevin de Bruyne, Gabriel Jesus, Leroy Sane

Unused subs: Claudio Bravo, Vincent Kompany, Nicolas Otamendi, Phil Foden

Booked: Sterling, De Bruyne

The first Premier League game of the season is exciting for everyone. The slate has been wiped clean and the records we'd set the previous season would mean nothing from this point onwards. Playing away at Arsenal is regarded by most players and supporters as one of toughest games of the season, and this match was being played just twenty-six days after the World Cup final.

Raheem Sterling scored his fiftieth Premier League goal to give us an early lead with an unstoppable shot from the edge of the box, and after that we controlled the game, though it took until the second half for us to get the crucial second goal that always creates a cushion. It was undoubtedly the biggest fixture of the Premier League's opening weekend and we'd shown that we were not going to rest on our laurels. We were up for the fight again.

Arsenal were making a fresh start in more ways than one. Unai Emery had succeeded Arsene Wenger, so there was a new hope among their supporters and there wasn't that familiarity about the way they would play. This was going to be a huge challenge. With Pierre-Emerick Aubameyang leading their attack, I'm told a lot of City fans thought I'd start the game in defence to combat his physique, but I had to settle for a place on the bench, which is always disappointing. They actually started well, but Raheem's goal seemed to knock their confidence.

I'm well aware that results at Arsenal for City down the years have not always been the best. It was something that changed a lot during my decade with the club, and in more recent times our performances have been excellent and the results much better. Games at Arsenal are always a huge challenge, but for this game we got it right and returned safely with the three points we needed. Bernardo had been playing very well from the moment he joined up with the squad in the USA and he continued to show his qualities in this game and swept home Benjamin Mendy's cross to complete the scoring.

In truth, we could have won by a wider margin and we dominated play. Pep Guardiola summed up the mood afterwards, when he said: 'Every season is a major season and this game was complicated, but we played at a high level. We created a lot of chances.'

Premier League (2)
Sunday 19 August
Etihad Stadium
Attendance: 54,021

MANCHESTER CITY	**6**

Aguero (25, 35, 75), Jesus (31), David Silva (48),
Kongolo o.g. (84)

HUDDERSFIELD TOWN	**1**

Stankovic (43)

City: Ederson, John Stones, Vincent Kompany, Aymeric Laporte, Benjamin Mendy, Fernandinho, Ilkay Gundogan, Bernardo Silva, David Silva, Sergio Aguero, Gabriel Jesus

Subs used: Riyad Mahrez, Leroy Sane, Phil Foden

Unused subs: Claudio Bravo, Kyle Walker, Nicolas Otamendi, Raheem Sterling

Booked: None

I was back in the team from the start for the home game against Huddersfield Town. I felt I'd had an unbelievable performance, in fact we all did. Sergio scored a hat-trick and everything clicked in the team. Huddersfield had drawn 0–0 against us towards the end of the previous season at the Etihad, so I guess this was a perfect example of Pep coming up with a different plan and it worked brilliantly.

The shape of the team was changed, with the two full

backs, Kyle and Benji, driving forward, which also allowed Pep to select both of his strikers, so it was Kun and Gabriel in attack. We could be as attacking as we wanted to be and I don't think Huddersfield had expected us to play that way.

David Silva scored our fourth goal that day with a superb free kick from the edge of the penalty area on his 250th Premier League appearance, and there to celebrate with him were his wonderful family and his little boy Mateo, the first time he'd seen his father play. That made it a very special day for us all, but I guess it will be the rampaging runs by Benji that people will remember the most from this game.

Despite feeling that I played well in this game and the emphatic win, I didn't for a moment believe that meant my first-team place was secure. It wasn't very long before my thoughts about the competition for places proved very real. I would keep my place for the next game, a trip to Wolverhampton, but I was very aware that if I made any mistakes John or Nico would be given a chance. When there are so many strong candidates to play, the pressure to perform is always high.

Kevin de Bruyne was injured in training in the build-up to this game. He had come back from his short summer break looking really fit. He was showing great signs of what we all knew he could do, but the incident that resulted in his injury was just a case of 'Kev being Kev'. He sometimes overstretches into challenges and he got caught accidentally and I think he went over on his knee. It looked worse at the time than it ultimately proved to be. We all thought, at that moment, that it was something that would rule him out for the season.

He's got natural quad strength and I think that helped

prevent more serious damage. The incident was just how Kev is. He can't help the way he is; it's one of the things that makes him so special. He goes into everything at full steam. He doesn't pull out of anything, even in training. He loves to nick balls away at the last second and that can sometimes create a bit of a tricky situation for him, but he can't change that and we wouldn't want him to.

Everyone knew that his injury would be a big blow to us. Any team would feel the effect of such a good player being out through injury. We had previous experience of losing players, of course, but the standards set by Kev are so high that whoever came in for him couldn't afford to be anything less than the very best they could be.

We needn't have worried too much, because as it turned out we got the best version of Bernardo Silva, and so many of the players who helped replace Kev in the team also played at their very best. That's a luxury that only a squad like City can produce. We had two full teams. It's difficult to say they're of equal strength, as each individual has so many different qualities and abilities. We know that Kevin has a fantastic range of passing, but Bernardo dribbles and moves so brilliantly into spaces.

Bernardo is very unlike Kevin in terms of what he can do, but the things he's good at make him exceptional, too. Another example of us having two teams might be that Gundogan is a very different player to Fernandinho. Gundo is extremely strong on the ball and knows exactly when to make a key tackle. Dinho can be very hard in a tackle when he has to, but his forward vision and long-range passing are good, too. They're top-quality players but with different assets. Each and every one of our squad is unbelievable at what they do, and can add something to the team because they bring qualities to the table that others can't. So, although we might have two players for each role, they usually provide different ways to fill that position.

Because Kevin is younger than me and we're both Belgian, I have to admit that I probably feel very protective towards him. We've played together on many occasions for our country, and I've seen how his performances have been reported by the media. Despite the beautiful football he plays, I believe he's been a bit unfairly treated sometimes in Belgium, especially around the big tournaments.

Inevitably, there have been situations where maybe he hasn't reached the same levels for Belgium as he has at club level with City. When that has happened, I've always felt the reaction was unfair. I've always wanted him to show to the world just how good I know he is, and I'm sure the City fans who watch him every week have no doubts about his qualities. I do look out a little bit more for him and I can't deny it makes me a bit happier when it's him that scores a goal. It's a rare thing for Belgium to have such a great amount of talent. I'm talking about Kevin, Eden Hazard, Romelu Lukaku; it's not normal for us to have so many great players in one generation. I want it to last and I want them all to do well.

Kevin is a quiet lad but he's got tremendous leadership qualities, especially during games. He's a winner. I would describe him as a big character on the pitch. Away from game day he's just one of the lads, joining in with all the jokes and all the fun stuff with the team. On the pitch, he's got that extra bit of bite about him, which is not always associated with a player of his talent. He's a bad loser, which is not necessarily a bad thing, but because we win a lot at City it's a great trait to have because we rarely see that side of him.

Back at City I've seen the jokes about Zinchenko looking like he is de Bruyne's son: a mini Kevin. If I had to describe the relationship between the pair of them, I'd say Kevin acts more like an older brother. I think Oleks sees the association with Kevin, especially when people joke that he's his father, as the biggest compliment he could possibly be paid. Kev just reacts to it by shaking his head. They both find it hilarious.

Oleks has such a nice personality, and it's been great to see him develop. He has turned into a very solid player. To have progressed so quickly and so well is incredible, especially playing in a position that isn't his natural one and for a very big team. You can only reach that level by having an amazing amount of desire and open-mindedness.

At the beginning of the season, it looked like he might be on his way out of City, that he was going to join Wolves or maybe somewhere else. Instead, he chose to fight for a place in our team and work with Pep Guardiola. It had seemed like he didn't have the right profile for the position he was playing in, but he proved a few people wrong by the end of the season.

There were many big games, and big moments within games, where things happened and we needed him. He just stepped up every single time. It was the same with Fabian Delph during the Centurions season, when he became one of the best left backs in the country. Zinchenko followed the same pattern. He got his chance because of the injuries sustained by Benjamin Mendy, which coincided with Fabian not playing so much. That shows what a great squad we had and that's what made us a strong team. Without these players doing what they did, it would have been impossible to become the team we were.

Premier League (3)
Saturday 25 August
Molineux Stadium
Attendance: 31,322

WOLVERHAMPTON WANDERERS   1
Boly (57)

MANCHESTER CITY   1
Laporte (69)

City: Ederson, Kyle Walker, Vincent Kompany, Aymeric Laporte, Benjamin Mendy, Fernandinho, Ilkay Gundogan, Bernardo Silva, David Silva, Sergio Aguero, Raheem Sterling

Subs used: Gabriel Jesus, Leroy Sane, Riyad Mahrez

Unused subs: Arijanet Muric, John Stones, Fabian Delph, Nicolas Otamendi

Booked: Kompany, David Silva

The game at Molineux was very different to the Huddersfield game. The team, me included, didn't play well but also didn't play badly. We drew 1–1, their goal being the infamous 'handball' from Willy Boly, and the next thing you know I was left out of the team for a month or so. That's how much pressure there was. It wasn't so much that I had done something bad and had to be replaced, it was simply that we'd drawn, so Pep's conclusion was that something must have gone wrong.

Football is a game of fine margins. We were one of the first big teams to play Wolves that season and I think everybody underestimated them. I said ahead of that game that Wolves didn't act like a small team and I warned that big sides would lose points against them. I called it early. They were not a Wolves team that were going to roll over. They proved to be very dangerous and went on to beat Chelsea, Spurs, Liverpool and United as the season progressed.

Wolves took the lead after a ball was crossed towards Boly, who threw himself full length to try to score. He couldn't connect with the ball in the way he'd hoped, but it went in off his arm. It shouldn't have been a goal, but the match officials allowed it to stand. After the game, Pep was asked whether VAR might have ruled that goal out and should it now be introduced to the Premier League. He simply replied, 'It's none of my business.'

What I remember particularly about that game at Wolves is that we defended a lot of very heated exchanges well, one-on-ones against very fast players. We were exposed a lot of the time, but we created so many chances and didn't capitalise on them, especially during the first half, and then we conceded that 'handball'. In truth, it was probably the only chance they had, apart from the one I gifted them, which they didn't take advantage of. I conceded possession to Moutinho, who countered on us and fed the ball to Jota. His cross to Raul Jimenez was perfect, but the forward tapped the ball home from an offside position. That's how close the margins are at this level. One mistake and it makes the headlines; it didn't even matter that my mistake hadn't cost us a goal. The fact was I made one error in the game, the team didn't win, and I paid the penalty by losing my place.

As far as dropping two points that day was concerned, we could have made all the excuses we wanted, but if we'd performed at our normal level we should have won that game. Despite that, we still hit the woodwork twice, we had a couple of penalty claims turned down and had the chances to win. On reflection, we were just the first of the big teams that failed to win against Wolves. As the season went on other good teams got a spanking by them. Only then would people realise they were actually a very good side. I could tell straightaway during that game how good Wolves were.

When it comes to my own performances, I'm a very self-critical person. I know I wasn't at my very best, but I certainly wouldn't have said that I'd had a bad game. As a top professional, I understand the high standards that players are judged by. If we'd won the game I don't think outside observers would have been quite as critical of my performance; after all I'd only made one mistake, and that hadn't led to a goal. But at City's level if you make a single mistake, people start saying things like 'he can't sort his feet out', as one reporter claimed, or 'he's too old'. That same reporter, a year later after a different result, might write something like, 'he's got his youth back'. I guess that's just how it goes. It's as if people wait for that one game when something goes wrong, when something dodgy happens, and suddenly the narrative is that you're fighting against the odds.

The result meant we ended August two points behind Liverpool and Chelsea, who'd both made a perfect start to their campaign. Despite convincing performances at Arsenal and against Huddersfield, we were chasing and we could already sense that this was going to be a tougher title race than it had been during the Centurion season.

CHAPTER 2

SEPTEMBER 2018

Premier League (4)
Saturday 1 September
Etihad Stadium
Attendance: 53,946

MANCHESTER CITY   2
Sterling (8), Walker (52)

NEWCASTLE UNITED   1
Yedlin (30)

City: Ederson, Kyle Walker, John Stones, Aymeric Laporte, Benjamin
Mendy, Fernandinho, Riyad Mahrez, Raheem Sterling, Sergio Aguero,
Gabriel Jesus

Subs used: Bernardo Silva, Ilkay Gundogan, Vincent Kompany

Unused subs: Arijanet Muric, Nicolas Otamendi, Fabian Delph, Phil Foden

Booked: None

Before this game I was presented with a framed shirt to celebrate ten years at City. Wow, that didn't feel like a decade of my life. It's moments like that when you briefly think back to the achievements you've had together with the fans. There were also flags flown in the crowd with my picture on, so it was a special moment for me. The only thing that really mattered though was winning again.

I made only a brief substitute appearance during the 2–1 home win against Newcastle. They came to the Etihad with the aim of keeping the score down, just as they'd done in the away game the previous season. It took a special goal from Kyle Walker to make sure of a 2–1 win, after Raheem had given us the lead. Kyle hit a superb low shot from outside the penalty area into the bottom corner.

Kyle admitted after the game, 'You could probably tell that it wasn't planned by the way I celebrated after the goal. My family is always up in the box and that was a big thank you to them because they'd stuck by me through the bad times and that goal had been a long time coming. I'm glad, with my first goal for the club, that I could get a vital one that got us the three points today.'

All wins are important, just like this one proved to be.

Kyle was my partner on the bus, he always sat next to me. In many ways, we couldn't be more different. He's all about his entertainment, his gaming, his music – that sort of thing. I was always thinking about managerial stuff and everything else going on in the rest of my life. Strangely, though, there's a middle ground where we sort of met.

Because of him, I had an unsuccessful spell on the online game Fortnite; and because of me talking to him, he started looking into his finances and the business side of his life a little bit more. We're miles apart from each other in some ways, but each of us have brought the other into our worlds a bit and learned off each other. When he finished talking about his entertainment stuff, I'd start talking about business. He'd show me his Fortnite videos and I'd show him my videos about how to invest his money. It was a really cool relationship.

As a person, he's one of those who gives you more back, in terms of your relationship with him, the more you give him. When he joined the club, he was stepping into big shoes replacing Pablo Zabaleta at right back. The one thing he did bring, which made it easier for us as a team as we got a little bit older, was raw pace. He has great power, too. He is such a dominant presence that he's already won his battle with whoever he is up against, before it's even played. That gives him a massive advantage. He creates a fear factor against opponents; he is able to blast through people.

He would be a big help to me, especially when I came back from injuries. For a long time, I took pride in being a lot faster than many people thought I was, which of course helps to make the game a little bit easier, but in those circumstances I think we complemented each other perfectly. I know I'd always been a fast player, but when recovering from injuries I couldn't overstretch myself. I had to be realistic and play within myself, rather than let pride take over and set out to prove that

I couldn't be outpaced – that might have led to a recurrence of the injury. Fortunately, Kyle was so quick he could temporarily cover my reluctance to sprint flat out, until I was sure I could do so once more without risk. I knew that I had Kyle there, just in case that ball dropped a little bit too far over my head. In that situation, I knew I would be okay because he had the pace to get in behind me and get the ball out of danger.

Premier League (5)
Saturday 15 September
Etihad Stadium
Attendance: 53,307

MANCHESTER CITY   **3**
Sane (2), David Silva (21), Sterling (47)

FULHAM   **0**

City: Ederson, Kyle Walker, Nicolas Otamendi, Aymeric Laporte, Fabian Delph, Fernandinho, Bernardo Silva, David Silva, Raheem Sterling, Sergio Aguero, Leroy Sane

Subs used: Gabriel Jesus, Ilkay Gundogan, Riyad Mahrez

Unused subs: Arijanet Muric, John Stones, Oleksandr Zinchenko, Phil Foden

Booked: None

After the international break, where I'd played in a 4–0 win over Scotland and a 3–0 win away to Iceland in our first games since the World Cup, I was rested when Fulham were next up at the Etihad Stadium. After Leroy Sane scored the quickest goal of the season so far, David Silva's half-volley was his fiftieth Premier League goal for the club. Raheem Sterling scored again just after half-time, on a day when Bernardo stole the headlines as he again showed his dazzling array of skills. After that, we seemed to ease off a little, ensuring everyone was ready for the start of the Champions League campaign on Wednesday.

Pep is a manager who thinks of squad rotation, which is understandable. There are other factors that necessitate a change of line-up too, like balance and the way the opponent plays. There were plenty of people who felt that, without Kevin in the team, we wouldn't be as good, and yet we still won almost every game. Those same critics would have argued that we'd have problems if we didn't have Fernandinho in the team, but we still won virtually every match during his absences, especially towards the end of the season. It was the same when I was missing games. Pep had created a machine with interchangeable pieces. This meant that when we had an injury problem, he was able to select the pieces that were going to solve that issue and last the longest.

Pep is a great coach and he is able to convince everyone that he is better than all the other managers and he can build a team stronger than all the other teams. He certainly convinced me and the rest of my teammates. He has a charisma that brings people on board and that makes everything he's trying to achieve seem easier.

Right from the start of his time at City, he had a lot of pressure on him to get results. It came from every direction. The fans expected a lot not only because of what he'd achieved at his previous clubs, of course, but also because of the finances that have been invested by the owners – so did everyone else. His reputation as a winner and the success he'd had in his previous jobs added enormously to the weight of expectation. There were also the demands from within the club: from us, the squad. We demanded results and he delivered. He got us ready for each game, giving us the right tools to be the best team every time.

I think he was very clever in the way he was able to give everyone enough game time to be part of this. Sometimes the changes he made were through his desire to freshen things up tactically, and on other occasions he was forced to alter the line-up when players were injured. Whatever the circumstances, and whatever changes he made from game to game, it worked and the results were consistently good. The team he selected almost always delivered because he had created this Rolls-Royce of a machine that could accommodate changes.

What makes him so good is the way he communicates, especially his tactics, in such a simple and straightforward way. It's the same in training as well. What he does is very clear. You'd be forgiven for thinking that anyone can do what he does, because it sounds very simple, but actually it's a very difficult skill to learn.

Pep definitely improved me as a player. As the season went along, I understood Pep's way of thinking more and more and the positions I needed to take, both in and out of possession. I believe he has done the same for every player in the squad. The biggest gift a coach can give a player is to help make them better. He deserves the biggest credit for that. Now I'm making the transition into management myself, it's what I dream of hearing from my players in the future. He's inspired other people to go into management, like him, and that's another big compliment to him. I don't see what more you can desire from a manager.

I remember Pep asking us all, quite early in the season, 'Do you guys still believe we can be champions again?' I was the first one to shout, 'Of course we can.' The main thing we needed to avoid was imploding or going into meltdown. Football is a sport of emotion, so when things start to go wrong, you can sometimes go into a quick decline. It's hard to stop the momentum unless you use your experience to overcome those feelings in key moments. Knowing what's happening, as it happens, has certainly helped me a lot. I've learned that staying calm is important in these situations.

Champions League Group Game (1)
Wednesday 19 September
Etihad Stadium
Attendance: 40,111

MANCHESTER CITY   1
Bernardo Silva (67)

LYON   2
Cornet (26), Fekir (43)

City: Ederson, Kyle Walker, John Stones, Aymeric Laporte, Fabian Delph, Fernandinho, Ilkay Gundogan, Bernardo Silva, David Silva, Raheem Sterling, Gabriel Jesus

Subs used: Leroy Sane, Sergio Aguero, Riyad Mahrez

Unused subs: Arijanet Muric, Vincent Kompany, Nicolas Otamendi, Phil Foden

Booked: Aguero

I think Mikel Arteta will be the natural successor to Pep whenever he chooses to go. He's been inside the coaches' room with Pep all these years, he's hungry and the City team has been built to play a certain way now. No one knows that system better than Pep, of course, but Mikel also knows that system inside and out. Whenever the time comes for Pep to take that next step and move on, it seems obvious to me that Mikel would be the one to replace him and if the players buy into it they'll have a great chance to sustain their success. I think it would be such an easy transition. There's very little to say against it. Who could be the next Pep Guardiola though? There's only one Pep.

Arteta sat in the coaches' dugout for the Champions League opener against Lyon because Pep was banned, following his actions after the Liverpool game in the Champions League last season. That group stage was a complicated one. Anyone that knows anything about the teams we faced – Hoffenheim, Shakhtar Donetsk and Lyon – knows that in terms of quality they were just a little bit behind City. I didn't think of any of them as being the equivalent to teams from the top four in the Premier League; rather they were like the ones just below, fifth to eighth kind of teams. Although this was a home game, I saw the strength of what we'd be facing as comparable, in terms of how difficult they would be to beat, with going to Everton away. Matches at Goodison Park were always very intense and challenging, but we still felt we had a decent chance of getting a result.

The games we faced in the group were the kind where you know it's going to be really, really tough, but one where the challenge ahead of us as players might be underestimated by the public. If we'd been playing teams like Barcelona, Juventus or Bayern, everyone would fully understand the size of the challenge. I think many people might see Lyon as being a weak team, which they certainly were not. Although they had not started the season particularly well, they had finished third the previous campaign. I suppose it was a bit like facing lower division opposition in one of the domestic cups. You're expected to win but get very little credit if you do, and so losing is not an option. That pressure when you're expected to win makes it even more difficult for the players because you have to guard against complacency.

Just as I'd expected, they proved to be very tricky opponents and they took the lead and added a second soon after, which meant we were 2–0 down at half-time, having twice been caught out by sloppy play in our own half. I'm sure that scoreline would have surprised a few people, but it just goes to show that there is little room for error, even in the group stage of the Champions League.

I can't imagine that Mikel had expected his first half-time team talk to be about how to turn around a 2–0 deficit. I suppose it was just one of those days, because who would expect Aguero not to take advantage of late chances after

Bernardo had reduced their lead to just one goal? After the game Mikel told the press: 'You have zero margin for error in the Champions League. If you make a mistake in this competition you get punished. We weren't at the races at the start of this game and we paid the price. I'm sure this team will respond in a very positive way when we play the next game in the group. Next time it will be a very different story. We'll be back.'

That's how we all felt; there were still five more games to play in the group stage, so plenty of time to make up for this defeat, but it was still very disappointing.

Premier League (6)
Saturday 22 September
Cardiff City Stadium
Attendance: 32,321

CARDIFF CITY	**0**
MANCHESTER CITY	**5**

Aguero (32), Bernardo Silva (35), Gundogan
(44), Mahrez (67, 89)

City: Ederson, Kyle Walker, Nicolas Otamendi, Aymeric Laporte, Fabian Delph, Fernandinho, Ilkay Gundogan, David Silva, Raheem Sterling, Sergio Aguero, Leroy Sane

Subs used: Riyad Mahrez, Phil Foden, John Stones

Unused subs: Arijanet Muric, Vincent Kompany, David Silva, Gabriel Jesus

Booked: Fernandinho

I watched the impressive 5–0 win at Cardiff from the bench with Riyad Mahrez sat alongside me for most of the game. That happened quite a few times during the season, unfortunately for both of us. Over the course of the season, I talked constantly to Riyad. I was telling him the same stuff I was always telling myself. You have to have this internal narrative and I naturally love to pass that on to other people as well. He wasn't a regular in the team at that stage, so I kept saying to him, 'All it takes is for you to curl one into the top corner and all will be well. Everything changes.' I told him to stay calm and that a lot can happen in a season: just wait and be patient.

We had these conversations all the time. He was insecure about whether he'd play again, about how the manager saw him. Even the fact that he'd signed for City from Leicester for £60 million, making him City's record signing and the most expensive African footballer, wouldn't guarantee him a starting place in Pep's team. While at Leicester he'd won the PFA's Players' Player of the Year award and had been a certain starter in almost every game.

At City it was different. I said to him, 'Look, he signed you for a reason; he has a plan for you, whether it's now or later, he's going to give you a chance.' I reminded him that the team was winning, winning, winning, so the decisions over team selection that were being made were fair. I told him to forget his negative thoughts and to concentrate on training, to get himself fit and to show the right attitude, to do the extra yards, go the extra mile and that would keep him at the front of Pep's mind.

I kept saying, 'He's looking for a response from you now, so he can give you a chance.' Exactly what I told him would happen did, and at the end of the season he got back in the team and we all know how important he was for us, especially in the Brighton game and that's what people ultimately remember.

Riyad is such a gifted player. He might not be as physically strong as some other players, but he's extremely talented. I always tried to give him honest feedback on where he was in relation to the team. Sometimes players, in fact people in all walks of life, make the wrong assessment of themselves and put themselves down a little bit too much. I would look at how he trained and be really honest with him. I would express my views in the right context and try to help him focus on what should be his ultimate priority. I told him to be ready for the chance at the right time, whenever it came. In the end, he got that chance and he was able to put himself in a position where he could compete.

It's hard for any player to come into a team that's just achieved 100 points and keeps going, steamrollering everything they come up against. In the game at Cardiff, he got his chance after an hour of the game when he came on for Sergio (who'd scored on his 300th City appearance) and scored twice. His first was a tap-in, but your first goal for any club is always crucial; his second was preceded by a lovely step-over and finished with a low shot, perfectly placed into the bottom corner. Those goals did his confidence a lot of good. After the match he told the press, 'I'm very happy to score my first goal for the team. It took a while to arrive but I knew it would come. I just want to help the team as much as I can.'

Despite having dropped only two points in our first six games, we were second in the Premier League, behind Liverpool who'd beaten Southampton 3–0 to complete six wins in a row. Already it was becoming clear that we weren't going to have the easy run we'd had the previous campaign; if we hadn't been aware of how tough the title race was going to be before, we understood how tight it might be now.

Carabao Cup Third Round
Tuesday 25 September
Kassam Stadium
Attendance: 11,956

OXFORD UNITED	0
MANCHESTER CITY	3

Jesus (36), Mahrez (78), Foden (90)

City: Arijanet Muric, Danilo, Nicolas Otamendi, Vincent Kompany, John Stones, Oleksandr Zinchenko, David Silva, Phil Foden, Riyad Mahrez, Brahim Diaz, Gabriel Jesus

Subs used: Raheem Sterling, Ilkay Gundogan, Adrian Bernabe

Unused subs: Ederson, Kyle Walker, Aymeric Laporte, Leroy Sane

Booked: Danilo

My next appearance was in the Carabao Cup at Oxford United. This was clearly a special night for Phil Foden, who played from the start in this game and scored a late goal to make the final scoreline 3–0. The Oxford game was one of those fixtures that people look down on. Just like the opponents we were due to face in the group stage of the Champions League, being away at League One opposition, midweek, meant we were on a hiding to nothing. We were expected to win comfortably, and didn't dare lose.

You know what? Those are the hardest kind of opponents. Everybody in the bigger club drops 10 or 20 per cent while the other team raises its level by a similar amount. If you don't follow your normal playing patterns and you lose discipline and individuals just start doing what they want to do, these games just get tough and silly. You start losing second balls, headers, free kicks, set pieces and the other team only needs something to go right for them and they suddenly believe they can win. These are dangerous types of games. Of course, we had younger players in our team that night, ones who didn't know the patterns we use in the first team, as well as those who played regularly.

What made me so proud that day was that it ended up being such a normal game for us. We prepared really well. I knew my role was bigger for that fixture; it felt like I was pushing even more than normal in that game. I pushed from the first minute to the last; in fact it started in the dressing room before the game. I wanted everyone to feel like this was a final. I knew that's how Oxford would look at it.

I reminded all the players before the game that the senior players had been smashing everyone in their path, week after week, so we (this team) had to go out and do the same.

We had no choice. If we were half-hearted it'd look bad, we'd look bad and it'd be used against us. As I remember it, we played a fantastic game. We should have scored so many times and the added bonus was that youngsters like Brahim Diaz, Phil Foden and Adrián Bernabé got their chances to play.

Phil scored his first senior goal for the club in that game, but, just as significant from my point of view, was that we got to see him play in a more liberated way for the first time, where he was just part of the team, not coming on for a few minutes and trying desperately to impress everyone. That night he was simply a major player in the team. Before that, he'd always come in and played second-string roles. We were all happy for him, of course. He's got talent and he's a Manchester lad, but that was the first time he could claim that he was one of the best players on the pitch for Manchester City. That's a big achievement for any player, in any game, wherever you play.

His reaction after the game when he was interviewed summed things up perfectly: 'It still hasn't fully sunk in but I'm happy to get my first goal for City but more importantly the win. I've dreamed about this moment since I was a kid and today it's actually come true. I tried to look for my parents in the crowd but I couldn't find them. Pep showed how much he believes in me and I can learn a lot from him.'

Premier League (7)
Saturday 29 September
Etihad Stadium
Attendance: 54,142

MANCHESTER CITY   **2**
Sterling (29), Aguero (65)

BRIGHTON & HOVE ALBION   **0**

City: Ederson, Kyle Walker, Nicolas Otamendi, Aymeric Laporte, Oleksandr Zinchenko, Fernandinho, Bernardo Silva, David Silva, Raheem Sterling, Sergio Aguero, Leroy Sane

Subs used: Riyad Mahrez, Gabriel Jesus, Phil Foden

Unused subs: Arijanet Muric, John Stones, Vincent Kompany, Danilo

Booked: None

I was back on the bench again for the 2–0 win against Brighton. Sergio was one of the goalscorers that day, as he has been on so many occasions during my ten years at City. I suppose when people look back on this season in years to come, they will forget this win against Brighton, or it will probably just be described as a routine win.

But there's no such thing as a straightforward win. When you score the goals you need to in order to beat the opposition, it might be concluded that it is easy. It isn't: to play well, either as a team or as individuals, takes a lot of effort, training, coaching and skill. For Brighton, like so many of our opponents, we knew this was a huge game and they certainly did not come to Manchester with the plan of rolling over and allowing us to win. When you are the Premier League champions, it seems that every team is extra motivated when they face you. Sides always get fired up when they take on the champions.

As a team we became used to controlling possession and people love to quote those figures to illustrate one team's dominance over another, but everyone who watches football knows that simply having more touches or time on the ball does not win you games. In this one, the goals that decided the game came from Raheem, on the counter-attack, getting on the end of a Leroy Sane ball, and through Aguero, who made a great run and then played a one-two with Raheem before finishing a quite magnificent move that had begun in midfield with David Silva.

The record books show that we won, but don't underestimate the efforts and qualities that richly contributed to this win, and many others like it. Take nothing for granted, always give your very best and don't come off the field knowing you could have contributed more. It was a win that saw us climb to the top of the Premier League on goal difference, because we played our game after Liverpool's draw against Chelsea. We now knew that when we went to Liverpool in our next league game, we'd have the chance to make a key impact on the season. September had been a good month, but some big challenges were coming up very soon.

CHAPTER 3

OCTOBER 2018

Champions League Group Game (2)
Tuesday 2 October
Rhein-Neckar-Arena
Attendance: 24,851

HOFFENHEIM   **1**
Belfodil (1)

MANCHESTER CITY   **2**
Aguero (8), David Silva (87)

City: Ederson, Kyle Walker, Nicolas Otamendi, Vincent Kompany,
Aymeric Laporte, Fernandinho, David Silva, Ilkay Gundogan, Raheem
Sterling, Sergio Aguero, Leroy Sane

Subs used: John Stones, Bernardo Silva, Riyad Mahrez

Unused subs: Arijanet Muric, Gabriel Jesus, Oleksandr Zinchenko, Danilo

Booked: Walker, Fernandinho, Aguero, Otamendi

I've played in Germany, so I knew what to expect at Hoffenheim. Everyone knows that German football is well organised tactically and the players of every team are well drilled and fit. There's also the atmosphere that's created in German stadiums, which always gives the home team a lift. What struck me about this Hoffenheim team is that they were great physical specimens who were full of running. Tactically, they played in a system that exploited their strengths. They played like no other team I've seen, with a line of five up front, all of them were constantly making runs, which is a real challenge for defenders. They were all over 6ft 2 tall.

We fell behind in the first minute of the game, which really focused our minds, but Aguero scored a goal to level things quite quickly. To come back, away from home when we had to win it, was a huge achievement for the team – psychologically it was massive. Then David Silva scored the late winner to secure a vital victory, as we would have been under real pressure to qualify if we'd failed to win either of our first two games. We could also have had a penalty, but our appeals were turned down. After the match, I commented: 'It's been a trend over the last six months, so hopefully that will turn around.'

When he spoke to the press after the game, Pep described David Silva as one of the best players he'd trained during his career. There's no doubt that David is a unique player. He's the perfect example of a player in his position. He started off as a winger and was incredible playing on the right side and cutting in, when he still had that pace. He was so clever in the way he chose where to perform and how to get into those positions, but then Pep later moved him into a more fixed position, in that pocket between the opposition's defensive and midfield lines. It took him to another level.

The particular quality that makes him stand out is that he is able to deal with any ball that you fire at him. He can work in the tightest space and he always makes the right decisions. It's such a unique skill he has, to be able to do what he does so well. As a manager, when I speak to my players or to other coaches I always talk with great enthusiasm about the number of midfielders who have a nice first touch and great technical ability; there are so many of them. You can even look at League One, the third tier of English football, and you will find these tidy midfielders there; everybody who watches those players know that they can also play well.

However, the difference between them and the very, very best like David Silva is still so vast, and it's all because of small but important details. David is so good at the way he receives any ball, even when there are opposition players all around him. He can work in even smaller spaces than those other technically gifted midfielders. In the next phase of his play, he then continues to make good decisions, quicker and more intelligently than almost anyone else I've ever seen. He loses fewer balls than them, too. If they lose two, he loses zero.

The timing of the pass, or when to make a supporting run to receive the ball – all things that might not always be immediately recognisable to the naked eye – these apparently small details make all the difference and are the reason he is so special. When I play alongside other midfielders, I can acknowledge their skill set and the abilities that they possess, but I still see such a big difference between them and David Silva.

Off the field, David faced a unique challenge during the Centurions season. Not only was he trying to play football at the very highest level, but at the same time he was dealing with the serious health issues being faced by his young son. Mateo was born prematurely at just twenty-five weeks' gestation and was fighting for his life in an intensive care unit in a Spanish hospital almost 1,000 miles away. I don't know how he was able to cope with a situation in his life like that.

While he was flying backwards and forwards to be with his wife and son, he wasn't really able to train with us in the way he would normally do. We knew that David was such an important player for us, so whenever he was back we were just happy to see him. He would go straight into the team and continued to play such an important role for us. He was on a completely different schedule to us in the way he trained and prepared for games. His particular situation required such a high level of game intelligence. That kind of preparation was far from ideal, and yet he was still able to perform consistently at the top level against top teams.

That's the measure of the man. It's more than desire or fitness, it's about understanding the game at a very deep level and about making the matches as easy for yourself as possible. I'm sure he wasn't always thinking as clearly as he normally would, nor was he in the ideal physical condition. It was perfectly understandable that his thoughts were often somewhere else. But you could not tell that if you watched him play. How he dealt with his wife being abroad and his kid being between life and death only he will know. As he reflects on what he went through, I'm sure he won't know how he coped himself.

We were so grateful for whatever he gave us during those difficult times because we really didn't expect anything. The way we looked at it, everything we got from him was a present, a bonus. We knew that we just had to support him, as friends. If we could do anything to help him, we would. We didn't want to intrude, but we were all constantly and discreetly enquiring about his situation. David is the type of person who would rather deal with those kinds of problems privately. He never asked for anything from anyone, so all we could do was wait and hope that everything would turn out well and that his little boy would be fit and healthy. It's at times like that when you realise what really matters in life.

It felt like a lot of what we did during my last season at the club was for him, for his son and for his family: a celebration for Mateo after all they had faced during the previous campaign. The story has a happy ending because, by the time we won the league at Brighton, David was able to celebrate those successes on the pitch with his son, which goes to show how far he'd come.

I know the City fans assume that the group of players that I came through with at the club are personal friends. That group includes David, Sergio, Joe Hart and Pablo Zabaleta, and there's certainly a great bond between us. As part of the teams that have won the league and had great success together, I suppose you could say it was an unspoken bond. It's because we've been on a journey together, we look each other in the eyes and we know how far we've come. It's a special relationship that will always be there between us.

Players have come and gone during my time at City, so there are different groups that have this special connection. Mine is with those of us who played together and won the first Premier League back in 2012, with Harty and the others, and I know it'll be the same between those who won the Centurions League. It's something you can't describe. We were there in that moment and there's a huge amount of respect between us.

I can't possibly put into words how much respect I have for David. The biggest compliment I've ever had was from David. He tried to convince me not to leave City at the end of the season. Sergio did the same. To have big players like them asking me to stay was absolutely the best thing for me. I played alongside them, but there're still heroes as well as friends and teammates. To have reached that level of respect from them is amazing.

Maybe people think that what I'm saying is to be expected or normal. Some might think that teammates would say that to each other and of course I've been a big player myself. The assumption is that everybody would automatically respect me. I don't believe that to be the case and I certainly don't look at it that way. To be respected by your colleagues, and such big players, is still something very special for me. I'm sure fans will also see this very differently than I do, because to them I'm a player the same as any other, but I've been excited to play in the same team as Aguero, Silva and the rest. They are special footballers. I just hope they think that way about me, too.

Until this point in my career, my story has been a weird

journey. I started at Anderlecht where I was viewed as the most exciting prospect in their pool of upcoming talent. During my time there we won everything, earning lots of trophies and personal accolades, and I was seen as the big rising talent. I then started to suffer from injuries, and life took a few twists and turns.

I had to graft more than the average player and I always saw myself as being the underdog. When you keep suffering injuries you are always having to prove yourself again and again. That's certainly how I felt. I started to think of myself very differently and in how I presented myself to the outside world.

It was important to me to push boundaries all the time. I saw myself as someone working hard behind the scenes. Some people might say that the injuries I suffered have helped keep my feet on the ground. I'd certainly like to think that they have made me more humble as a person and that I appreciate the successes I've had that little bit more than some others do. It's also why I have dealt with all the setbacks I've had so well, because I have always been so grateful for anything I have achieved. I felt like I was constantly starting from a losing position. City fans can probably relate to that more than anyone else!

I've suffered a huge Achilles tendon injury, and the damage I sustained to my thigh in the Champions League semi-final at Real Madrid while at City was described by the medics as looking like my leg had been hit by a bullet from a shotgun. When they opened it up, they asked me how I had walked off the pitch. It was like my leg had exploded. Yet I still have it in my head that if I could have finished that game I could have had an influence on the eventual outcome. We lost that one 1–0, of course. Maybe that helps explain why I always see myself as being the underdog.

I was still recovering from that horrendous injury when Pep was announced as the new City manager. I believed at the time that he would have preconceived ideas about me. The fact that I was injured and had this record of sustaining injuries made me wonder if this would always be at the front of his mind. I assumed he must have heard that Vinny 'always has injury problems, he's always injured' – those kinds of thoughts. I must have been on the treatment table for the first two or three months of his time at City, recovering from what happened in Madrid, so I was completely out of the picture and his planning. When I was fit again, I believed I had to work and fight to be part of his plans; I didn't assume anything. I think having that attitude helps in sport, and elsewhere.

When you're constantly battling back from injury, you always feel like you're an underdog. Not being part of the team is frustrating; no player wants to be outside the group. It's happened to me far too often during my career. As a result, I've never taken my involvement in the big occasions for granted. Similarly, being among big players and behaving like a big player was something special for me. All the good things that have happened to me, and that I have been involved in, have been a bonus for me.

And the win in Germany was certainly another positive; it had put us back on track in the Champions League after the defeat to Lyon, so the mood in the dressing room was full of confidence as we moved on to the next big challenge: the trip to Anfield.

Premier League (8)
Sunday 7 October
Anfield
Attendance: 52,117

LIVERPOOL	**0**
MANCHESTER CITY	**0**

City: Ederson, Kyle Walker, John Stones, Aymeric Laporte, Benjamin Mendy, Fernandinho, Bernardo Silva, David Silva, Riyad Mahrez, Raheem Sterling, Sergio Aguero

Subs used: Gabriel Jesus, Leroy Sane

Unused subs: Arijanet Muric, Vincent Kompany, Nicolas Otamendi, Danilo, Phil Foden

Booked: Mendy, Bernardo Silva, Aguero

We knew how significant this fixture was and, because of how close the title race was proving to be, we knew that losing was not an option. The mood among City fans towards these games against Liverpool had changed. They'd always been seen as tough fixtures but now there was more tension. They knew, like we did, what was at stake.

I was on the team coach when it was bricked going to the Champions League game at Liverpool the previous season. The moment that happened, and especially because of the way it was so poorly organised for us to get into the stadium for a big match, things changed between City and Liverpool. The rivalry increased and they became our number one team to beat. To give them some credit, they had also become the hardest team to win against.

It's not just what happened on the way to that game that changed my view of them. There have been lots of key decisions that didn't go our way. There have been penalties not given, offsides that should or shouldn't have been awarded – all that kind of stuff. There was the goal that was ruled out in that second leg in the Champions League, when Leroy Sane's tap-in should have been allowed. All those incidents had an effect on how we viewed playing against them and increased the intensity of the rivalry. To be honest, though, sometimes good rivalries are built on those kinds of controversies.

On the day the coach was bombarded on the way to the Champions League quarter-final, I thought that it might have given us the edge. None of us were sitting on that coach saying that we were scared. We just thought and said to each other, 'All right, let's sort it out on the pitch.' It didn't work out that way, though. Whatever the reason, we just weren't there on that day; we didn't play like we knew we were capable of.

Although it was very unpleasant, and should never have been allowed to happen, I don't think the coach incident made any difference to the eventual outcome of the tie. We played them at home and lost as well, and we played them in the league at Anfield that season and we lost that game, too. They'd just been a difficult team for us to handle. In the Champions League game, I think every chance they had was converted into a goal, which is very rare in football. It was just one of those days. We had forty-five bad minutes.

Our second-half performance was actually very good, but people forget that because of the result.

For this visit to Anfield, the fixture had increased in intensity and of course there was added importance on this one because of the title race. We felt we had a point to prove. I could see that it was becoming a deep rivalry, especially because of how things were turning out. What had happened the year before actually gave us a bit more motivation this time. Watching from the bench, I felt that our performance was comfortable during the game, even though we ended up with two more points dropped. Naturally I was disappointed not to be playing in the game, but then again everyone who's not selected always feels that way.

These are the types of matches when you have to put your own frustrations about not being selected to one side. It's a squad game and every bit of help you can give your teammates, especially those who are playing, is important. The key thing is City, ideally, winning the game. The fact I wasn't on the field was secondary in that situation.

We took a more cautious approach to this game and, although I believe we deserved to win, the plan would have worked perfectly if we'd managed to score a late goal – and we had the chance to do just that, after Virgil van Dijk brought down Sane. Unsurprisingly, most of the headlines after the game were about Riyad Mahrez missing the penalty that followed, sending it over the crossbar, but that didn't bother us because the media plays such a small part in our consciousness as players. We're very well insulated from them at City. We just get on with things. For us it's more about our relationship with each other as players, and the relationships with the coaches, rather than worrying about what was said in the papers.

We knew this was a big game, and Riyad was the one who stepped up to take the penalty, as Sergio had been substituted by then. You could feel the added pressure on Riyad as he took the spot kick. I have great respect for any player that's prepared to take on the responsibility in those moments. If you miss a crucial penalty like that, you've got to deal with the consequences. He knew that it could go wrong, but he still stepped forward. Riyad deserved praise for that. At the end of the season when the trophies were handed out we won the league, so the fact that he didn't score that day didn't matter. Instead, right at the end of the season he helped us unlock the Brighton game and that's all that matters.

Aymeric Laporte had a great game that day and I'd describe the way in which he was integrated into the team as very smart. He arrived in January 2018 and played thirteen games during the second half of his first season. At the beginning of the 2018–19 season, Pep made the decision to trust him, no matter what. As a young player I think you need the manager to give you that trust and the feeling that you're going to play in most of the games. Eventually, and especially because he was part of a great team, he was able to go from strength to strength and impose himself as one of the leading centre backs in the league. He made fifty-one appearances in all competitions, missing just ten games all season.

To give him that time was clearly a strategy because Pep believed he was going to reach the level that he needed to. It proved to be a smart plan because he has become so consistently good and now he is at a very high level. From

City's perspective, he's got so many more years when we can expect him to continue at that standard.

I think he has a very different profile and skill set than I have. He has an incredible amount of self-confidence. As a result, he never seems to panic and he's got a very good eye for the right pass, which sometimes is even more important that the quality of the pass. It's a case of making the right pass at the right time and he does that very well. His cross-field passes are exceptional and I think that shows why having a left-footed centre back on that side is so important to Pep. The accuracy of his diagonal passes adds to his qualities as a defender and gives him that extra edge.

The way he played at Anfield during that vital 0–0 draw summed him up as he helped ensure that they didn't create any real chances in the entire game, which was a huge achievement. He got lots of praise for his performance that day and on many other occasions throughout the season. Coming back to Manchester with a point proved to be a good result and showed that we were capable of adapting to the situations we faced in games.

Pep put things into perspective after the game when he told the press, 'We've had forty or fifty years of not winning here and often we've lost. This is a good result, I'm so satisfied with what we have done. As a team you know Liverpool will punish your mistakes and at the back we controlled it very well. It would be better to win at Anfield but we didn't lose, maybe next season we will win, we will see.'

With eight games now played, Liverpool, Chelsea and City all remained undefeated, only the second time that had happened in Premier League history. Was it going to be a three-horse title race? As we left Anfield that day we certainly knew that there wouldn't be much room for error during this season.

Premier League (9)
Saturday 20 October
Etihad Stadium
Attendance: 54,094

MANCHESTER CITY	**5**

Aguero (17), Bernardo Silva (54), Fernandinho
(56), Mahrez (83), Sane (90)

BURNLEY	**0**

City: Ederson, John Stones, Vincent Kompany, Aymeric Laporte, Benjamin Mendy, Fernandinho, Bernardo Silva, David Silva, Riyad Mahrez, Sergio Aguero, Leroy Sane

Subs used: Kevin de Bruyne, Gabriel Jesus, Phil Foden

Unused subs: Arijanet Muric, Nicolas Otamendi, Oleksandr Zinchenko, Raheem Sterling

Booked: Sane, Kompany

After the Liverpool game, there had been another international break, where I'd played in Belgium's 2–1 win over Switzerland before watching the 1–1 draw against

Netherlands from the bench. I was back in the team against Burnley, a comfortable 5–0 win at the Etihad Stadium. I know I hadn't played every game but when my chance came again, I certainly knew what to expect. I never suffered from nerves. I'd been in this type of situation so many times down the years.

What I remember most about this match is that in the first minute or so I got a poor ball across the back line that was going straight to Aaron Lennon's feet. I had two choices. Either pull out, which would mean he'd be through on goal, or just do what good defenders do and make sure he wasn't getting past me, if I couldn't take the ball off him. I admit that my challenge was a bit hard, but I had no choice but to stop him and I took a yellow. What other decision could I make? Either way you're not going to get a victory lap out of it. If you analyse the situation in detail, the problem was the bad ball. The focus afterwards by most of the media and fans was on what I did to try to correct it. I did what I needed to do.

I would never deliberately try to hurt an opponent. Winning the ball and preventing a goalscoring opportunity is the only thing going through my mind. The Burnley manager, Sean Dyche, felt I should have had a red card for that challenge. All I can say is that I was a ball winner throughout my career and my challenge that day was honest and with no malice intended, so I thought the yellow card was the right punishment.

We created lots of chances on top of the five goals we did score. I remember Harty, who was in goal for Burnley, pulled off so many great saves, otherwise the score could have been even more emphatic. I don't think I lost one header against them, which I was pleased about as they were a physically big team. Throughout the game we probably had about 70 per cent ball possession and completely dominated.

This was one of Benjamin Mendy's sixteen appearances during the season. Benji is the kind of character that everyone wants to do well. He might seem flashy to some people, both on and off the field, but in reality he is someone who has had to deal with a lot of adversity in his career. He's had very difficult stuff to cope with, including big injuries and recurring injuries. Anyone who's been through that sort of thing, like I have, understands the amount of work that goes into the battle to get back to full fitness.

There's nothing better than seeing a guy who's having to go through this kind of hardship eventually returning to his best level. That's what I'm hoping for with Benji. Every single day that I have watched him, I'm amazed by how he can keep up that level of happiness. Despite the face he shows to us around the club, and the one the fans see, I know that somewhere deep down his only focus is to get back on the pitch, fully fit, and to return to the level we all know he's capable of.

My wish for him is to get out of the spiral he's been in and to write his name on some of the trophies that City will win in the future. He's had a cruciate ligament rupture, thigh problems, a knee surgery, a foot injury – the list goes on and on. I want him to not only be part of the team but one of the leaders of the future. That's the next step for him. He still has all the tools to do that. That path is a tough one and all we hope for is that he gets to the right end of it as soon as possible so he can really enjoy what he's good at.

Even though he missed many games through injury, he still contributed richly to our success. This was a season where we achieved ninety-eight points and yet we only beat our closest rivals by one point. Anybody that put their boots on and played made a massive contribution to what we achieved. In his case, he's the type of player who can reintegrate very quickly, but he might also need a bit of time and understanding to get him back to where he was before those more recent injuries.

He certainly brings positivity into the dressing room and onto the field. He has a huge role in that sense, because football is not just about tactics and great players, it's also about having a positive impact on the players and the team around you. I think he spent a lot of last season being a bit introspective, working out what the new him would be, and whether he needed to be a different sort of player. I've been in those injury situations many times, so I know what it's like not knowing if you'll return the same as you were before. There may have been occasions when he's twisted and turned without thinking. Once he's back to full fitness this autumn he might have to think more, taking into account his body's weaknesses and play less instinctively. It's unlikely he'll be the same player when he eventually returns. It doesn't mean he'll be less than the player he was, so think of him as a 2.0 version of Benjamin Mendy. For now, the important thing is to go through the process.

Champions League Group Game (3)
Tuesday 23 October
Metalist Stadium
Attendance: 37,106

SHAKHTAR DONETSK	**0**
MANCHESTER CITY	**3**

David Silva (30), Laporte (35), Bernardo
Silva (71)

City: Ederson, John Stones, Nicolas Otamendi, Aymeric Laporte, Benjamin Mendy, Fernandinho, Kevin de Bruyne, David Silva, Raheem Sterling, Gabriel Jesus, Riyad Mahrez

Subs used: Bernardo Silva, Kyle Walker, Phil Foden

Unused subs: Arijanet Muric, Sergio Aguero, Leroy Sane, Vincent Kompany

Booked: Otamendi

A few days after the Burnley game, we went to Shakhtar, where conditions were difficult, and won with a very convincing performance. It kept up the momentum of all the good things we were doing. Pep used the words 'outstanding' and 'incredible' to describe the way the team played, particularly during the first forty-five minutes when we went 2–0 up. It was the first time Shakhtar had been beaten in Europe at home by an English team. Pep went on to say, 'By winning in Germany and here we have recovered from the defeat against Lyon and things are in our own hands again. After that defeat against Lyon, we were under pressure but today we played really good.'

The Ukrainians were very well organised with good discipline, so we had to play really well to beat them, even though it proved to be comfortable in the end. We created lots of chances, with Riyad Mahrez pulling a shot wide and having another blocked. David Silva hit the post before he drilled in a low shot to give us the lead. Later in the game the chances kept coming before Aymeric Laporte added the second and Bernardo, who'd only just come on with twenty minutes to go, scored the third. The result put us top of Group F and back in control of our own progress to the knockout stage of the Champions League.

It never ceases to amaze me how great City fans are. As a club we are playing more and more games a season, with Champions League football now a regular thing, and yet there were still hundreds of supporters with us in Kharkiv. That sort of loyalty and commitment makes a win feel all the more special, and it's something that, as a player, always helps to spur you on.

Premier League (10)
Monday 29 October
Wembley Stadium
Attendance: 56,854

TOTTENHAM HOTSPUR	**0**
MANCHESTER CITY	**1**
Mahrez (6)	

City: Ederson, Kyle Walker, John Stones, Aymeric Laporte, Benjamin Mendy, Fernandinho, Bernardo Silva, David Silva, Riyad Mahrez, Raheem Sterling, Sergio Aguero

Subs used: Kevin de Bruyne, Vincent Kompany, Gabriel Jesus

Unused subs: Arijanet Muric, Nicolas Otamendi, Phil Foden, Leroy Sane

Booked: Laporte, Fernandinho

I didn't go on in this game until the last few moments at Wembley against Tottenham. We won 1–0, thanks to a goal by Riyad Mahrez, but it was a difficult match, there was no doubt about that. Just as there was no doubt this was such an important one for us. I've talked about the significance of fine margins in games, and if Erik Lamela had taken advantage of our mistake and scored instead of putting it over the bar when he was in a clear position, that could have changed the whole dynamic of the fixture.

Lots of things were not right for that game. The playing surface was certainly not in a good condition. There had been three consecutive NFL games played on it, the latest being only twenty-four hours before this important Premier League game, and this had resulted in a rutted track right down the middle. It was cut up and uneven and made it very difficult for us to play our normal passing game. The pitch was a disaster, and I don't think I'm revealing anything to other clubs when I say that we lose a significant percentage of what we're all about on surfaces like that. That's natural.

Later in the season, we went to Burnley and they seemed

to have dried the pitch as much as they could and let the grass grow a bit longer because they thought they could gain an advantage from doing that. We were and are a team that thrives on the speed of movement of the ball. Every club tries to provide playing conditions that are best suited to their team.

We simply had to accept those conditions at Wembley and do what we needed to do to win the game. It really wasn't something any of us were comfortable with, and I'm sure it didn't help Spurs much, either. On the positive side, we trusted in each other as a team and I always knew that there were players who could do something special in these moments; something you wouldn't expect.

The match was played at Wembley because Tottenham's new ground was still not ready, but I accepted that because ultimately you have to support progress. If delaying their move back to the new White Hart Lane was what they had to do to get over the line with the new stadium, so be it. That's how the Premier League became the Premier League, because they have progressed and clubs have improved. As long as other clubs are allowed that flexibility to do the same thing and go through the same phases in their development, it's fair.

Funnily enough, I studied the importance of home advantage when I did my thesis for my Master's in Business Administration and the conclusion I came to was that playing your first games in a new stadium should in fact be a disadvantage to the home team. When we later played them in the Champions League at their new stadium, it should have helped us that day. The fact that they were in a new facility on a new pitch should have evened things out in our favour, because the home side loses the aspect of familiarity. But it didn't work out like that, did it?

Fernandinho had one of his typical games that night at Wembley. He's an outstanding player as a defensive midfielder. He was very special to us every time he played. Sometimes people forget what a good footballer he is and how good his football brain is. What I love about Dinho is that he has that ability to catch people up on long breakaways. If the other team are suddenly on the counterattack, and are running at us, he has the ability to make up the yards and snuff it out. He'll then recycle the ball.

Like most great players, he always stepped up to an even higher level when it came to the really big games. It's as if he can spark off things around him, too. The way I see it, it's like when there are suddenly a few drops of blood in the sea. It creates a reaction straightaway. It sends sharks into a feeding frenzy. He's the one who starts that off and it's very effective. You could always rely on him. He was never frightened of letting his opponents know he was around.

People often think of Brazilian footballers as being highly skilled but not always the strongest. It might be a bit of a cliché, but it's certainly a common perception. Dinho doesn't fit that description. He certainly has plenty of natural technical skills, but he can also be as tough as anyone else when he needs to be. There are other Brazilians like him of course, but they are usually full backs and those types of positions. The other thing about him is that there's such an honesty about his work. He has played in plenty of other positions for the team, showing the kind of versatility that John Stones has, but you can never find fault with him. He never has a bad game.

At times, it felt like Pep went to the extreme with Fernandinho and seemed to deliberately play him in every position, but only Dinho could have adapted to each one thanks to the wonderful ability he has.

He's older than me, but I can see him being around at City a while longer yet. Under Pep I could imagine him being capable of playing as a centre back. That change of position might not work for him if he was at another club, but the way Pep sets up his team, I think he could play there very effectively. He can retain the ball, he's got good athleticism and he can win his challenges. As long as the opposition is not sending torpedoes into the box for sixty minutes of the game, I think he could play anywhere.

That's not to say his days as a number six, the holding midfielder, are over. There is a tradition of players in that position carrying on to an older age, so there's no reason he can't be a key player in his defensive midfield role for quite a while yet. He knows, as well as I do, that with age we all have to adapt, and of course the signing of Rodri, soon after I left City, will offer him another challenge. As it was, during last season it was Ilkay Gundogan who usually played in the holding midfield position when Dinho was absent, and he's not the fastest player in the world, which shows that playing there is more than just speed over the ground. It's far more complicated than that.

The win took us to twenty-six points and kept us top of the table only on goal difference from Liverpool, but we had already played three of our biggest rivals away and picked up seven points out of nine in them. Chelsea were two points further back, with Arsenal also in the mix on twenty-two points. There was no scope for error.

CHAPTER 4

NOVEMBER 2018

Carabao Cup Fourth Round
Thursday 1 November
Etihad Stadium
Attendance: 35,271

MANCHESTER CITY	**2**
Brahim Diaz (18, 65)	
FULHAM	**0**

City: Arijanet Muric, Danilo, John Stones, Vincent Kompany, Oleksandr Zinchenko, Fabian Delph, Kevin de Bruyne, Phil Foden, Brahim Diaz, Gabriel Jesus, Leroy Sane

Subs used: Riyad Mahrez, Claudio Gomes

Unused subs: Ederson, Kyle Walker, Bernardo Silva, Raheem Sterling, Sergio Aguero

Booked: Kompany

I remember the Fulham game was another big one for Phil Foden. This was an opportunity for him to play more meaningful minutes to add to those he got against Oxford in the earlier round. Before those games, he'd been getting time on the pitch mainly just for the sake of getting minutes. I think that Oxford game was the start of the next phase of his career.

Phil is perfect for Pep's system because he's an ideal pocket player. The manager likes to have that kind of footballer who can turn and drive. It's one thing to be able to receive the ball, turn and pass, but he's able to receive, turn and drive at the back line. Not many players can do that and then pick the right pass and arrive in the box. He's not fazed by the physicality of the game, no matter how much he lacks physicality himself.

He's got everything to become one of the main players of Pep Guardiola's era. The only thing he needs to do now is to work hard and secure a permanent place in the team. That's the hardest part. Young players are sometimes treated differently to the more senior pros. Sometimes the way it has to be done seems a bit unfair on the others, but you have to give them chances to play, to give them a path and to create opportunities for them, otherwise they'll never be at the level of the other guys.

I played alongside John Stones and Nicolas Otamendi in this game. It was a rarity for us to play three in the middle. I saw that a tackle I made on Timothy Fosu-Mensah in that game was described as him running into a lamp post. I'll take that as a compliment. I absolutely loved playing alongside John, I think he's the full package; he's unique. He's got incredibly good feet, but he also has light feet. He can play short passes and he's a natural when he comes into midfield, which tactically gave our team another advantage. He can go into the right-back position. He's got a decent enough left foot to play all the passes as well. He's quick and mobile, which means he's very versatile at the back and plays well in whatever role he is given.

He's definitely improved his strength to come out on top in challenges, which was probably what he struggled with the most at the beginning of his time at City. He's progressed very well, and in a really natural way. The injuries he's had to deal with have been unfortunate, and with such fierce competition for the centre-back positions that never makes things any easier.

It was certainly not impossible for him to play alongside me on my left, but that's not really the ideal way for him or me to play. From a personal point of view, I always enjoyed playing in the same team as him, despite the potential problems that caused, simply because we're both right-footed. He's a very coachable player, he listens and he hasn't got any sort of arrogance about him.

When it comes to Nico, well, what can I say? He is what he is. He's a warrior. He's clever, he's a veteran. He's one of those guys who knows how to do the job, no questions asked. There's no doubt that one of the strengths of our team was to be able to name all these guys, top-quality players, for one position. If you think about that, it's ridiculous.

You could ask John, Nico and me at any time whether we wanted to play more games, and of course we would all say yes. It didn't really matter what combination was selected by Pep, each pairing was incredibly strong and we all got lots of minutes on the field as the season went along. Our strength came from unity and quality.

John sees himself first and foremost, as a centre back, even though there were occasions when he played in the holding midfield role or even at full back. When I was coming through the youth system at Anderlecht, centre back and defensive midfielder were interchangeable. The two positions were seen as roles that could be constantly swapped around.

The player driving into midfield stays in midfield, with the midfielder dropping naturally into the centre-back position. As a result of that flexibility, during the early part of my career I played 50 per cent of the time in each position. It meant that as I developed my game, it felt completely natural for me to swap roles within games.

In hindsight, I was just a player who loved to run and tackle people. That was the aspect of football that I really enjoyed. I had the ability to drive past people and get away from the challenges that might come in. I had good instincts and I could dribble, but the one thing that was probably missing from my game was having the 360-degree vision to play in small areas. That changed when I met Pep Guardiola.

When I first moved to City from Hamburg, I wouldn't say I saw myself as either a midfielder or a centre back, even though I'd played in more of a midfield role there, but the thought of limiting myself to just being a centre back might initially have seemed a bit restrictive. I realise now that I could never have been as good as Fernandinho in midfield. The great strength of Fernandinho is that he thinks defensively, but also from an attacking perspective. It's like he has eyes in the back of his head. He seems to be aware of everything around him. That makes him very special. I wasn't that type of midfielder, but I could have been a good, solid defensive midfielder. I needed someone to teach me when to turn and when not to turn. I kept turning into traffic when I was playing that position earlier in my career, and you can't afford to make those mistakes at the very top level.

The best thing for me was to drop to centre back where I was a lot stronger. The reason I never enjoyed centre back in the early days was that I never had the framework of a good defence around me. I always felt that I was correcting other people's mistakes when I was in that role. Perhaps that feeling was encouraged by how the game was viewed back then. When you watched TV highlights, it was always the defenders who got singled out for criticism. It was always the goalkeeper or the defenders who were blamed for the goals conceded. You never saw the person in midfield who lost the ball being highlighted or an emphasis on what led to the attack starting.

Back in the day, it was a case of freeze-framing the moment the ball goes into the defensive area and then the analysis would be, 'This defender is not in position, or that player should be there.' Hold on a minute, you can't defend with just three or four players, you need the whole team to defend. That frustrated me. These days, certainly when you watch *Match of the Day*, they've started to analyse games differently, but it didn't happen like that so much when I was starting my career and deciding where I wanted to play.

At City that changed when Mancini came in. He started to build a very tactically organised and disciplined defence, with the whole team involved in the process, and I actually started to understand what the strength of a defence was. If you were well organised, it made such a difference. I then started to really enjoy defending.

I always enjoyed one-on-ones; I relished those challenges. But when I came to understand what it meant to just focus on defending as a team, I started loving it. From that point I completely made the transition in my head and I thought, *I'm done with midfield.* I now wanted to be the very best I could be as a defender. I needed that sense of 'it's a brotherhood', and under Mancini that was the first time I'd experienced it.

Brahim Diaz grabbed the headlines by scoring both goals, and I could almost claim an assist for the first one. The young Spaniard, who moved to Real Madrid halfway through this season, had been at City since 2015, making his first-team debut in September 2016 against Swansea. He is an attacking midfielder who loves to dribble, but he'd struggled to get in the side – and when you saw that Riyad, Bernardo and Raheem were on the bench, it was easy to understand why.

Another injury concern for Kevin de Bruyne meant there was also a downside to this game. Kevin hobbled off near the end with another knee injury, after Fosu-Mensah landed on him. Players want to play games, win matches and ultimately win trophies, so those who say that playing in these cup competitions is risky are wrong. Kev's previous injury problems came as a result of a challenge in training, so things like that can happen any time. The most important thing was that we were through to the next round of the competition.

Pep refused to single out Diaz for particular praise and said he didn't know the extent of the new injury to Kevin:

'It was an excellent performance in terms of how we were without the ball. We were aggressive when we needed to be. We gave the competition the respect it deserves and we created enough chances to score more goals. We are not thinking about trying to win the Carabao Cup back to back, we just tried to win this game and go through to the next round.'

Premier League (11)
Sunday 4 November
Etihad Stadium
Attendance: 53,916

MANCHESTER CITY   6
Hoedt o.g. (6), Aguero (12), David Silva (18), Sterling (45, 67), Sane (90)

SOUTHAMPTON   1
Ings (29)

City: Ederson, Kyle Walker, John Stones, Aymeric Laporte, Benjamin Mendy, Fernandinho, Bernardo Silva, David Silva, Raheem Sterling, Sergio Aguero, Leroy Sane

Subs used: Vincent Kompany, Phil Foden, Fabian Delph

Unused subs: Arijanet Muric, Danilo, Riyad Mahrez, Gabriel Jesus

Booked: Aguero

Liverpool's draw the previous day at Arsenal meant that we would go top of the league by two points if we won our match against Southampton. It turned out to be a comfortable home win during which I came on as a substitute in the second half, so I think it's fair to say that everything was going along very nicely indeed. While many in the media were acclaiming our performance and the flair of our forwards, Pep didn't ignore the fact we'd conceded a goal he thought we shouldn't have given away.

It was one of many games during the season where Raheem Sterling showed us exactly what he was capable of. He scored two of the six we bagged against the Saints and helped set up three more. There had been a time in Raheem's career when he wasn't really appreciated in the way he deserved to be, particularly by England fans. We always knew how good he was, so this performance was a reminder, if he needed to give one, of the full range of his skills.

Now that I'm a manager myself, I often talk to my younger players about the way that Raheem has developed his game and improved as a player. He's a great example to my young wingers. We always knew what a great talent he was, but he's also one of the most improved players, from one season to another, that I've seen in many years. I've seen few players develop as quickly as Raheem has under Pep.

He was very different when he first came to the club in July 2015. He was young when he arrived from Liverpool, but the way he has learned in those few years has been amazing. He has increased his effectiveness as a player so much. Talent can take you to a certain point in the game, but ultimately you are also judged on numbers, on how many assists you create and whether you are able to perform in big games. That side of things was always up in the air with him. We knew he could do it, but there have been so many young players down the years that we had expected to progress but who did not. Progress and development should not be expected; they need to be learned.

Suddenly we've seen Raheem switch into another gear. It's as if something just clicked in his head and he understood how to make the game easy for himself. Youngsters who work out how to make football easy become big players. His transition was really interesting to follow, and that's why I now use his story as an example to help educate the young players in my team at Anderlecht.

Ultimately, to succeed at football you have to be able to figure out what you need to do to reach your goals. Raheem has done well to tap into his own personal drive to improve so spectacularly, but also to take the advice of one of the best coaches, if not the best in the world. From within the City camp, his story has always been interesting to follow because not only has he developed as a player but he's pro-gressed as a human being. There have been times when he has been portrayed badly in the media by people who don't know him or can't relate to him. This is just not right and not fair.

There were suggestions that he was treated like that by his critics because of racism. I do think that the media is some-times quick to create a perception and jump to conclusions without really knowing someone. If anything, from what I have seen, they should be using Raheem as an example to all young people. He comes from a rough neighbourhood, but he's well educated. He's got very good values and he looks after the people he loves. He's his own man and has his own personality. He has had to deal with tremendous amounts of glory and success, but he has done this in a very humble way. He's young and he likes to have fun, too. What more could you want from someone, if he's being successful?

I think that the first step to making this right is for those people to understand where the other person comes from and how they see the world. Unless an effort is made to understand that other world, they'll never be able to portray someone fairly. That has been my issue with the way Raheem was treated and it was particularly noticeable at the beginning of the season.

If you don't have any diversity in your organisation, then you're never accountable to anyone. An unrepresentative organisation can never see things from a different perspective. A lot of progress has been made over the years in terms of players from different origins getting access to playing the game. In other walks of life, such as the mainstream media or music, there are plenty of people from all sorts of backgrounds. The connection all those individuals have is that they're talent driven. Cream rises to the top when it's purely based on ability. If you're a great singer and people like your music, you succeed, regardless of race or background. However, within many organisations I don't feel that getting to the top is always purely talent-based in the same way.

I think those of us from diverse ethnic backgrounds have been able to earn our place in areas where ability is easy to define (if you're a centre forward, you will be judged on the number of goals you score and create, not on the colour of your skin), but it's a very different situation when you look at who is in the boardrooms and the areas of unseen power. They're basically the people who have control over what goes on and who gets what jobs. They're the hand you never bite, because they're the ones that feed you. We're not in those places, so we'll always be pawns on the agenda rather than setting it. That's a big issue for me.

Champions League Group Game (4)
Wednesday 7 November
Etihad Stadium
Attendance: 52,286

MANCHESTER CITY   **6**

David Silva (13), Jesus (24, 72, 90), Sterling (49), Mahrez (84)

SHAKHTAR DONESTSK   **0**

City: Ederson, Kyle Walker, John Stones, Aymeric Laporte, Oleksandr Zinchenko, Fernandinho, Bernardo Silva, David Silva, Raheem Sterling, Gabriel Jesus, Riyad Mahrez

Subs used: Danilo, Ilkay Gundogan, Fabian Delph

Unused subs: Arijanet Muric, Nicolas Otamendi, Sergio Aguero, Leroy Sane

Booked: None

I wasn't involved in the Champions League game against Shakhtar, but we swept them away with another impressive win. The most notable incident in the fixture came when Raheem Sterling hit his foot accidentally into the ground, fell and we were awarded a penalty. If I look back at it now, from my position as a manager, in an ideal world I would prefer not to have the penalty. I'd want things to be fair in every instance, however. You can't be the only team that holds up your hands and tries to play with a higher integrity than everyone else; everyone else has to as well. Ultimately, you can't leave yourself in a position where you're giving an advantage to those who are not as honourable as you are. I think football needs to create an environment where honesty doesn't disadvantage your team.

Moving onto the Champions League itself, every time we played in the competition in recent years, the City fans have booed the UEFA anthem. I can understand why they do it and I think it can be traced back to the game we played at CSKA Moscow when City fans were banned. We'd played at CSKA in 2013, when Yaya Toure was the subject of racist chanting, and by the time we played them again a year later the game had to be played behind closed doors. (In theory.) Yet it was the home fans that were meant to be banned as a punishment for racist booing or chanting. My first reaction to that was, why could our fans not go to that game? What had they done wrong? I couldn't understand why a game being played behind closed doors couldn't include the City fans. Why could they still not enjoy an away game?

I'm not saying that all fans of CSKA were responsible for what led to that punishment, but the club had to take ownership of what happened and suffer the consequences. Why not reverse the fixture or play it on a different ground where City fans could still go to the game? There had to be a solution that didn't punish both sets of fans.

The second issue I had with what happened was that the game was not in fact played behind closed doors. There were about 500 of their supporters in the stadium, which was meant to be empty. The excuse was that the sponsors were still entitled to attend the game because it was in the Champions League, which falls under the jurisdiction of UEFA, and they said that it was only the 'normal' fans that had to be banned.

All I can say is that the sponsors over there must be very different from the sponsors who attend games elsewhere in Europe. They acted like fans. They cheered like fans. It became hard to believe that this was supposed to be a game in an empty stadium. We had no fans in that stadium. You can spin it any way you want, but the way I look at it, the team that was disadvantaged from that game being played 'behind closed doors' was City. It was a shambles. The team they were supposed to be punishing was the team that gained the advantage on the day by having some fans to cheer them on.

The other major reason City fans boo the UEFA anthem is the introduction and administration of 'Financial Fair Play'. FFP is such a tricky subject to tackle. Trying to make clubs financially healthy is an important thing. I get it. When it comes to competitive balance, I've never agreed with it. If you're an established top club and you inherited your position because of whoever had ownership or the controlling position before you, that's one thing. Does that make them the rightful clubs to stay at the top, for ever, because they did things the 'right' way? That's rubbish.

They had someone funding them, whether it was twenty years ago or fifty years ago, or even one hundred – that's what happened almost everywhere. There'll always have been one guy or one company who pumped in a bit more money than everybody else. It doesn't matter which club you are. There might be one exception to that rule somewhere out there, but for the vast majority of all the clubs who've got to the top of the tree, that's how they've done it, somewhere in their history. Big industries and very rich individuals funding them to gain an advantage. Once they've established their position they want to lock it in with an FFP rule that makes sure that the prescribed order remains.

In my opinion, City breaking into that group was like a breath of fresh air for football. If you are already the biggest club with the most fans, you will naturally always have the biggest turnover and that gives you the ability to buy the best players, so how the hell is that status quo ever going to change unless someone can come in with a vision and a plan and invest?

Of course, we need to get to a stage where football clubs are healthy and able to function without the concern that they could collapse. I certainly believe in transparency, but I don't believe that FFP offers that at all at the moment. It's nowhere near what it should be. Transfers should be totally transparent, along with everything else that happens within a football club, because the stakes are so big.

It doesn't matter whether you're just a taxpayer or you're a fan, you get emotionally attached to a club, a league or to the game itself. It's such a high-profile sport and enter-tainment these days that it demands to be run in the right way. When it comes to the funding of growth, I think that's what makes progress possible. If you look at the whole pic-ture of what City has done and will do in the future, as a club but also as a business in Manchester, it's phenomenal.

Some people underestimate what Manchester City has done for the city of Manchester. Manchester United have made a difference, too. These two clubs have put the city on the map. You can go anywhere in the world and tell them you are from Manchester and they will know where it is and that there are these two huge clubs there. If there was no City and United, there would be many people abroad who would hardly know the difference between Manchester and Hull.

I don't think some people know what a big boost to the economy it is to have such giant footballing superpowers in what is quite a small city like Manchester. It's an area that needed that sort of economic push. Do people real-ise the amount of money being pumped into the city of Manchester from outside the country? It's an area and a league that might not normally have come into contention for something like this. I'm not saying everything about it is perfect, but it can enable progress.

I believe that if you make a financial commitment to invest and to boost a club to a certain level, that should be your right as an investor. What should happen is that there ought to be a compulsory part, in terms of the com-mitment that the investor makes. If you say you want to commit £100 million, then you should have to do this for a certain period, maybe five or ten years. That way you enter a long-term contract and you can't just pull out and leave the club in a financial mess. That way every club that finds an investor has long-term security and some stability. Too often of late we have seen people come in with big promises to invest, only to depart soon after leaving their clubs saddled with massive debts.

To avoid such problems, when this investment ends clubs need to have a scale-back plan that allows things to go back down without any damage to the infrastructure and is linked to the contracts or the values of the players. That way you avoid a fire sale because the club has got into financial difficulties and needs money quickly to survive.

I don't think it should matter where the money comes from, as long as you can trace it to an owner that is reliable and passes all the due diligence checks. If you pass that type of scrutiny, I don't think it should matter how much anyone wants to invest. I don't think how an owner has actually financed the club should matter. We should simply support it. The question should be, 'Have they made a long-term commitment? Will they suddenly decide next year that they no longer want to put any more money in?' That's completely different.

If someone wants to commit £500 million per year for the next decade, why stop it? Despite all the investment that has come in, City have not gained an advantage over the biggest clubs in the world; that money had to be brought into the club just to catch up with them. It's certainly not a case of us wanting to kill the competition.

As a result of all this I can understand why City fans boo the UEFA anthem, but I also think that if we really want to win the Champions League we should start the competition with every positive attitude possible. Until, as a club and its fans, we're sure that we want to win this league more than anyone else, we don't deserve it. If we don't really want to win it, then we shouldn't.

I think most people will agree with me that that's fair. I'm sure that we're ready to put this behind us and deal with it in another way or at another time. I don't quite know where and when that will happen, but I do understand that for City fans it must feel that during the playing of the anthem is the only time and place they can voice their opinions. All I will say to them is this: I know what it's like to be a player on the pitch trying to have a positive, energised feeling from the moment you enter the pitch, and I'm not sure that hearing your fans booing the anthem helps with that. Everybody needs to be pulling in the same direction. It should be about the team, first and foremost.

Premier League (12)
Sunday 11 November
Etihad Stadium
Attendance: 54,316

MANCHESTER CITY   3
David Silva (12), Aguero (48), Gundogan (86)

MANCHESTER UNITED   1
Martial (58)

City: Ederson, Kyle Walker, John Stones, Aymeric Laporte, Benjamin Mendy, Fernandinho, Bernardo Silva, David Silva, Riyad Mahrez, Raheem Sterling, Sergio Aguero

Subs used: Leroy Sane, Ilkay Gundogan, Phil Foden

Unused subs: Arijanet Muric, Vincent Kompany, Fabian Delph, Gabriel Jesus

Booked: Bernardo

The Manchester derby was always special to me. I'm married to a Manchester girl and, as you no doubt saw on the Amazon documentary, my father-in-law is a red, so that always makes it extra-special when we play them, or should I say when we beat them, as we have had a habit of doing in recent years. Although I haven't forgotten that the last league defeat I played in for City was the United game at the Etihad Stadium the previous season, which delayed our coronation as champions.

I was an unused substitute for what proved to be my final derby at the Etihad Stadium. It was a comfortable win, though neither team played the football we've been used to from them in recent years. It seemed to me that United had given up the fight at that point. Their season hadn't started well and they didn't look like a happy team. It wasn't really a game. We did the job, we were better, we won, but you need two to tango.

I suppose that's why Liverpool became such an intense rivalry for us, because they have been trying to match everything that we were doing. They've tried to add pace and power. For so long, United had been full of pace and power, but this certainly wasn't the case in that game. I do remember thinking as the match unfolded that we got a little bit too comfortable. We didn't move the ball as quickly as we had been doing. After the game Pep pointed that out to us, saying we should hold ourselves to a higher standard, no matter what the opposition does.

I can't say I was disappointed that the game wasn't as good as it could have been. Winning a derby was traditionally always so important to me, indeed perhaps the most important thing. We won the derby quite easily and that's all that mattered that day. I'd never come away from a win in a derby feeling disappointed; never, no way. The derby the year before had been intense enough, so I much preferred the outcome of this boring derby.

This was, though, let's not forget, the game where Ilkay Gundogan finished off a forty-four-pass move to make the scoreline 3–1. Much was made of that third goal, but for us that move was bread and butter. We always had that in us. I'm saying it as if it's normal, but Pep has been able to create this sort of football everywhere he's gone over the years, so the overwhelming feeling was that if we wanted to achieve what we wanted to achieve we had to hold ourselves to a higher standard in the overall performance.

I remember clearly that we all felt that way after the game, despite the win. It was after that game that we started to dip in form a little bit and having high standards is what helps you to avoid those situations. We knew that at certain moments during that game and the matches that followed, we had left ourselves open to things that didn't need to happen. That was certainly one of those games, even though it proved to be comfortable in the end.

We'd known what we needed to do before that game

and how we wanted to approach it, but we didn't do everything perfectly. It's maybe difficult to understand that from the outside, but I think every player in the team knew and remembered. Don't get me wrong, we were all very satisfied with the result, simple as that. I think it's fair to say that we won that game with something to spare. I'd describe this as a smart performance, rather than a great one.

Premier League (13)
Saturday 24 November
London Stadium
Attendance: 56,886

WEST HAM UNITED 0

MANCHESTER CITY 4
David Silva (11), Sterling (19), Sane (34, 90)

City: Ederson, Kyle Walker, Nicolas Otamendi, Aymeric Laporte, Fabian Delph, Fernandinho, Ilkay Gundogan, David Silva, Raheem Sterling, Sergio Aguero, Leroy Sane

Subs used: Phil Foden, Riyad Mahrez, Gabriel Jesus

Unused subs: Arijanet Muric, Vincent Kompany, Oleksandr Zinchenko, John Stones

Booked: None

I didn't play in the 4–0 win at West Ham, but I was on the bench as we faced a team managed by our former boss Manuel Pellegrini and which included Pablo Zabaleta. Both of them, quite rightly, received great support from the City fans who travelled that day. I played with Pablo for such a long time. He's like a City monument but somehow he is walking around another place or another club. I still see him as a City player who's just being loaned to West Ham for a couple of years. I could see him wearing the West Ham shirt, but it didn't really connect with me. It felt like he was wearing the opposition kit for a bet and that he'd change back to his City kit later. Obviously I've played against former teammates many times, but Zaba was a bit different because we shared a dressing room for such a long time.

Manuel is like every manager who's brought success to a club. He'll always be associated with a very important part of all of our stories. Watching him working with the backroom staff at West Ham gave me a special feeling. You can't afford to be sentimental in football, so the reality is that whatever good times you've had together, you sometimes have to face your friends in opposition. It might have felt strange, but we desperately wanted to win, so for the ninety minutes of the game all we focused on was beating West Ham, not on their manager or who was playing in their team.

I have learned things from every manager I've played for and every teammate I've played alongside, so I look back on the experiences I've had and try to take the positives into the situation in which I now find myself. Under Manuel, we attacked with so many players. It was a very tough system to play in as a defender. With Pep the way we attacked and defended was very balanced. You attack with five players and you defend with five, roughly speaking. When you analyse it afterwards, you can say that everybody attacks and everybody defends, but when you look at it on paper there are two very distinct functions within the team. There are those that create and score chances and there are those who defend and recycle the ball. With Manuel it felt like everyone attacked.

Only two players were out-and-out defenders under Manuel's system, the two central defenders. Our job was to make sure that the other team didn't score whenever they broke us down. That system felt a little bit crazy at times, but for the strikers it was brilliant. It showed what kind of a team we were then, particularly during the first six months of Manuel's time at City. Those were such good times, right up there with any of my experiences playing at City.

We played in an offensive 4–4–2, with Negredo and Aguero up front and Dzeko on the bench. We had so many attacking players. There were Nasri and David Silva running riot. Fernandinho was still a very offensive player in those days. Yaya Toure sprayed the ball around, charging forward like only he could, and we had attacking full backs: Zaba was going forward all the time on one side and on the other it was Clichy or Kolarov, so it was the most attack-minded, daring football I'd ever seen.

I learned the aspect of full attack under Manuel, but I also learned what the potential pitfalls are of playing that way. It's difficult to control games and it's difficult to impose your style of play for ninety minutes against big teams that deprive you of possession. Under Manuel, when we played against Pep's team we got decent results. I remember us beating Pep's Bayern Munich 3–2, thanks to a hat trick by Aguero. It was tough, though, because we couldn't recover the ball. We generally relied on moments of genius, as having control of the game certainly proved more difficult. In simple terms, it was all about attacking under Manuel and as far as I'm concerned it was a special period to play in and be proud of.

Statistically, we were very close in his title-winning season to our Centurions season or this English treble season. We scored 102 top-flight goals in 2013–14 under Manuel, the Centurions reached 106 Premier League goals and during the 2018–19 campaign we bagged 95. The big difference is that we relied a lot on the individual ability of defenders to plug the gaps, whereas under Pep it's the system that takes care of it.

Winning 4–0 away from home, especially in the Premier League, is always something to be proud of. It's probably fair to say that we weren't at our absolute best, but we played very well and came away with a comfortable win.

This was the first City game for a fortnight, following the third international break of the season when Belgium had beaten Iceland 2–0, but then lost 5–2 against Switzerland after being 2–0 up after seventeen minutes, thanks to Eden Hazard. After our victory, Pep said, 'Sometimes after the break you don't quite have the rhythm, but we came back and immediately after just one training session we travelled here. My players have quality. The four goals were fantastic, the performance was incredible especially after an international break. I don't care if we score more

'He played a big role in the things we achieved at the club' – Kevin de Bruyne and I on a visit to the Royal Manchester Children's Hospital in December.

When I got back to City after the World Cup and a seven-day holiday, my main focus was to be as ready as possible for the start of the season.

Although I didn't start the game, I came on as a substitute in the Community Shield and was able to make some good tackles, as here against Victor Moses.

A 2–0 win over Maurizio Sarri's Chelsea was a great way to start. Pep Guardiola was on top of us from the start of the season, with a series of new rules, to make sure there was no complacency.

Arriving at the Etihad for our first league game of the season, as we set out to defend our title. The match couldn't have gone better: we beat Huddersfield 6–1.

Holding off Diogo Jota during our game against Wolves, which finished 1–1. We saw immediately what a strong side they would be, having just been promoted.

Being presented with this shirt to mark ten years at City was a special moment – but I could not think where the time had gone.

Ilkay Gundogan leaves the field with an injury during our 2–1 victory against Hoffenheim. During that match, David Silva (right) once again showed why he is a unique player.

Despite the 5–0 scoreline against Burnley, City legend Joe Hart pulled off so many great saves to stop it being an even bigger win for us.

Organising the defence during our 6–1 win over Southampton in November. It was typical of Pep that he didn't ignore the goal we conceded.

Rising above Troy Deeney in our hard-fought 2–1 win in December.

Celebrating with Oleksandr Zinchenko after Sergio Aguero scored the goal that gave us a 3–1 lead at Southampton going into the break. We'd lost our previous two games, so this victory on 30 December gave us a boost after we'd dropped behind Liverpool in the title race.

Our 2–1 win over Liverpool at the Etihad in January was played with more intensity than any other game I can remember – more importantly, we closed the gap with them to four points.

I'd been disappointed not to start the Carabao Cup final, but, when Aymeric Laporte picked up an injury, I ended up relishing almost ninety minutes of action, facing up to my Belgium teammate Eden Hazard.

After some drama over who would be in goal for Chelsea during the penalty shoot-out, we emerged as the winners and could celebrate again.

goals this season than we did last year. The danger to my players is that they read lots of nice things about their performances, so we push each other a lot. We know that Liverpool won again [3–0 at Watford] and for a club with such a history, we know how tough this fight for the title will be.'

He wasn't wrong about that.

Champions League Group Game (5)
Tuesday 27 November
Lyon Olympic Stadium
Attendance: 56,039

LYON   2

Cornet (55, 81)

MANCHESTER CITY   2

Laporte (62), Aguero (83)

City: Ederson, Kyle Walker, John Stones, Aymeric Laporte, Oleksandr Zinchenko, Fernandinho, David Silva, Riyad Mahrez, Raheem Sterling, Sergio Aguero, Leroy Sane

Subs used: Fabian Delph, Phil Foden

Unused subs: Arijanet Muric, Brahim Diaz, Vincent Kompany, Nicolas Otamendi, Danilo

Booked: Fernandinho, Sterling

Although I didn't play any part in the game in France, we were all very aware that getting the right result there would help us to come to terms with what had happened in the first game between the two teams in Manchester. The home defeat had got us off on the wrong foot, and this performance against a very good French team helped to put things right. The draw we achieved also guaranteed we were through to the knockout stage. We now only needed a draw against Hoffenheim at home to win the group and avoid some of the more highly rated teams still in the competition when it resumed in the new year. Shakhtar had snatched a late 3–2 win at Hoffenheim while we were drawing at Lyon, so the job was completed for now.

Lyon were second in the French league when we played them, and Pep said they were 'one of the toughest teams we've ever faced. Physical, strong and their counter-attack was incredible.' That made our performance and result in France all the more impressive and kept our confidence levels high as we prepared for the games to come.

We came from behind twice, which showed a mental strength to our squad. Having lost the home game against Lyon, it might have put doubts in our minds when they took the lead, but both times we recovered. Pep described us as having 'a huge personality. We did it, which shows we are strong in these situations. We are into the last sixteen, which was complicated in this group. People say the French League is just Paris St Germain, but they are so wrong. Always in my career French teams are so physical. That's why they are World Cup winners.'

December was always going to be a very challenging month, with lots of fixtures coming in and around the

Christmas period. Happily, for at least one of those games, the home tie against Hoffenheim, the pressure would largely be off, but there was no respite in the Premier League race.

CHAPTER 5

DECEMBER 2018

Premier League (14)
Saturday 1 December
Etihad Stadium
Attendance: 54,409

MANCHESTER CITY	**3**

Bernardo Silva (16), Sterling (57),
Gundogan (79)

BOURNEMOUTH	**1**

Wilson (44)

City: Ederson, Danilo, Nicolas Otamendi, Aymeric Laporte, Oleksandr Zinchenko, Fernandinho, Ilkay Gundogan, Bernardo Silva, Raheem Sterling, Gabriel Jesus, Leroy Sane

Subs used: Fabian Delph, David Silva, Riyad Mahrez

Unused subs: Arijanet Muric, Kyle Walker, Phil Foden, Vincent Kompany

Booked: None

We were at the start of a period of thirteen games in forty-four days, so there were matches coming every three days, which meant lots of squad rotation. For this game, Aguero was missing with a minor problem so it was a chance for Gabriel Jesus to lead the attack. We won the game 3–1 and I suppose when people look back through the history books at this one they'll assume that it was just another straightforward win, but they rarely are. The football didn't flow as freely as it did on our best days, partly because of the number of changes that were made, but also because Bournemouth didn't come simply to hand over the points.

You get into a rhythm in football, so I guess it's inevitable that making changes can sometimes alter the dynamic of the team, but, as always, with the quality we had in the squad there was plenty to enjoy about this game. Once again, the passing was controlled and a joy to watch, with Ilkay Gundogan showing us the full range of his abilities. Two players stood out for their attacking qualities. Raheem Sterling and Leroy Sane went on mesmerising runs, but the truth is that with the score at 1–1 Bournemouth had a good chance to take the lead. However, I was so confident with the team that even if they'd gone ahead we would have turned it around and still won the game.

Pep said he had not been worried and admitted that for

the latter stages of the game, the last twenty minutes, we had been flat but he also said that was normal because of the number of games we were playing. During November we'd played six games: three of them in the Premier League, a Carabao Cup tie and two group matches in the Champions League. But that was nothing in comparison to December, where this was the first of nine scheduled in the month. As long as we were winning we remained two points clear at the top of the table, with Liverpool continuing to win their games too.

I've spoken about the competition for places in defence, but with Leroy and Raheem playing like that plus David, Bernardo, Ilkay and Riyad all competing for places in the team, you could see what Pep was doing. Despite plenty of games coming up, which would allow squad rotation, no one was guaranteed a place. They had to be at their very best.

Premier League (15)
Tuesday 4 December
Vicarage Road
Attendance: 20,389

WATFORD   1
Doucoure (85)

MANCHESTER CITY   2
Sane (40), Mahrez (51)

City: Ederson, Kyle Walker, John Stones, Vincent Kompany, Fabian Delph, Fernandinho, Bernardo Silva, David Silva, Riyad Mahrez, Gabriel Jesus, Leroy Sane

Subs used: Ilkay Gundogan, Nicolas Otamendi, Aymeric Laporte

Unused subs: Arijanet Muric, Danilo, Phil Foden, Raheem Sterling

Booked: Ederson

I was back in the starting XI for the away win at Watford, a game which saw Leroy Sane score the opener in a 2–1 win. This was a tough match. We dominated, we had lots of possession and I wouldn't say we had any problems, but I suppose we struggled to break them down at times. This wasn't the only time that finding the crucial breakthrough was tricky, but eventually Leroy and Riyad scored and we got our lead. It was a narrow victory in the end, with them getting a goal back late on, after we'd dominated so much. These types of games are the dangerous ones where mistakes can happen, things can go wrong, but we got the win, so I didn't need to try a spectacular shot from outside the box in that one. I saved that for another day.

I love Leroy as a person and as a player. I speak German, of course, which helps, but to be honest I've always had a great connection with him. I'm sure that to those who don't know him like I do, he might seem like someone who's so laid back that he's not really bothered about things, but actually he's always hungry for information and cares a great deal about everything that's going on around him.

He fully concentrates and pays attention to everything.

He's very self-critical and a very honest person, which might surprise some people. I find it so rare for a professional footballer to be as honest as he is with himself. When he has a bad game, he'll accept the criticism, but actually he'll probably beat you to it and be the first to say what he should and shouldn't have done. Sometimes he'll be too harsh on himself.

He's the type of person who you don't really connect with unless you know him well. He's a player with exceptional pace and when he's at the top of his game, as he was at the start of the season, he is unstoppable. His runs are not just quick, they're powerful and he goes all the way. There are other players who are fast over a certain distance, but not always right through to the end of a move. He starts moving forward fast and finishes even stronger.

Confidence is a key part of any player's skill set. Some need blind trust and then over time they just get better and better. They need a run of games and then they get fully into their stride, while others are fine just getting minutes here, there and everywhere. Take Bernardo Silva, for example. It doesn't matter if you give him twenty minutes or whether you give him ninety minutes every game, he's always very close to his potential. But Leroy, like most players, needs more of a run of games. With the competition at City and all the quality players fighting for first-team places, that's not always easy to achieve, as I saw myself.

Under those circumstances any player can get into a spiral where it becomes easy for spectators to mis-analyse a situation and assume he's not having a good time. It's just that some need more time on the field, and that's probably true of Leroy. When he has a run of games he never disappoints and he looks like an unbelievable player. He made a huge contribution to the season; everyone did. It's crazy to look back on it as being about what happened in the last few months. We had to start strong and finish strong to end the campaign with ninety-eight points, one ahead of Liverpool. Anyone who stepped foot on the pitch during the season was extremely important, including Leroy, who scored a vital goal in this game and made many other highly significant contributions.

This was a game where we saw the best of Leroy, tormenting and bewildering Watford at times. The last few minutes of the game, as Watford pushed for an equaliser, may have caused some anxiety for our travelling supporters, but we came away with another win.

Premier League (16)
Saturday 8 December
Stamford Bridge
Attendance: 40,571

CHELSEA	**2**
Kante (45), Luiz (78)	
MANCHESTER CITY	**0**

City: Ederson, Kyle Walker, John Stones, Aymeric Laporte, Fabian Delph, Fernandinho, Bernardo Silva, David Silva, Riyad Mahrez, Raheem Sterling, Leroy Sane

Subs used: Gabriel Jesus, Ilkay Gundogan, Phil Foden

Unused subs: Arijanet Muric, Danilo, Vincent Kompany, Nicolas Otamendi

Booked: None

All had been going exceptionally well until this point in our race for a second successive Premier League title, with just the two lots of dropped points at Wolves and Liverpool, so we went to Chelsea full of confidence, unbeaten in our first fifteen games. We played well at Stamford Bridge, but just didn't take our chances, which proves my point about the fine margins that decide the outcome of matches. I was an observer from the bench for this one, and I knew that as soon as we lost, as we did at Chelsea, I would get a proper chance again.

I'd learned that in this team it was all or nothing. I'm not sure if I was the only one who felt like that. No one ever solves the problem on their own, it's a team game; but if you can't work out a solution to the problem immediately, if you're not lucky enough to be part of a winning team as soon as you're back in, then you're out. I knew that had been my situation for the last few years at City.

I am naturally a fighter. What people might not realise about me is that I'm at my best when I feel like my back is against the wall. I have a natural venom that goes through my veins; something kicks in, I suppose it's adrenalin. I actually feel an excessive amount of calmness and strength when I'm in this position. That was exactly what happened to me during that season. Every single time I felt I had to prove everything again.

It was this ongoing fight to prove myself as being worthy of a place in the City team that eventually led me to the conclusion, *I'm going to have to leave.* That's why I made the decision to move on from City. I couldn't help thinking to myself that I'd been a bit lucky to still be able to compete for a place. I was getting older and there were plenty of top-quality players who deserved to be in the team. I thought perhaps that the next time, or the time after, I might not be so lucky and work my way back in again. That's normal – I was fighting against younger rivals for my position and up against tough opposition so I found myself playing less and less; those things don't match well. I didn't want to be in the team thanks to sympathy, especially now that I'd had everything I'd dreamed of. That's why I started to think my time at City was coming to an end, even though I hadn't made a final decision at this stage of the season.

I've always known I was good, it's never been in doubt, but I'd got to that age where it felt like if I had one bad game people would start thinking, *he's done.* I realised that I'd surfed on top of that wave for long enough and one day they might just be correct, so it became the right time to say my goodbyes in the best fashion possible.

Liverpool had beaten Bournemouth before we played, so we knew that anything but a win would leave us trailing. We had a couple of chances in the game, but we didn't take them, and when Kante scored for Chelsea it felt like it had come against the run of play. Having plenty of the ball doesn't count for anything if you don't score goals, and we couldn't find the net in this game. For the first time in a while, we were behind in the title race.

For all that the result was an important one, and had a

bearing on the title, the game at Chelsea was also significant for another reason. It was the day that Raheem Sterling suffered verbal abuse from a couple of individuals in the crowd. He didn't need to get involved with these idiotic people, so he didn't. He smiled at them, which is really difficult.

No one knows how they would handle a situation like that until it happens to them; it can bring out emotions that sometimes you can't control. We're not just talking about skin colour here – you could come from a village that has suffered due to the decline of the coal industry and you're verbally abused. It could be that your abuser doesn't know the significance of the word they have used. It could be a derogatory term about the village you were from or about the mine you'd worked in. Without knowing all the facts, your abuser might make a specific reference to a name or word that you'd been called that in some way denigrated your people. Being on the receiving end of that abuse is terrible and had it been the other way around they would feel very differently.

Racism is basically about this. If you call someone a certain name and his culture and background has suffered from that stereotype, then you should understand that the person won't accept it. That they will have a very strong reaction to it. For Raheem to stay calm in this situation is to be admired. Many couldn't. He handled it in such an important way. He was able to make it about the issue rather than the emotion.

I've been in that position as well and I'd like to think that given how often I've had to deal with it, I've found a way of controlling myself in the moment and not reacting. I'm not saying we shouldn't put pressure on organisations to sort it out, for there should be appropriate punishments handed out to help to eradicate this type of behaviour. What I'd prefer to do though is to tackle the higher issues, through being part of those that set the agenda, being in the boardrooms where the big decisions are made behind closed doors. That's where you can really make a difference and have an impact.

I was looking at UEFA and their anti-racism campaigns. The entire UEFA committee numbers around 100 members with not one person from a BAME background on it. An organisation that wants to deal with racism hasn't got rep-resentatives sitting on the board able to put this issue in the right context or to speak from direct experience. Just think how many issues there are in football and society that we all talk about where we don't have the right representation. That's what I'm concerned about. The two guys who abused Raheem aren't the problem, however wrong what they did was. The bigger problem is that the system judging the two men, and others like them, has no idea what Raheem could feel like in that situation.

Unless you sit down with people, seriously, you'll never get the right level of understanding. Listening is the key and not just choosing your words to suit your agenda.

If I'm your boss, in any work environment, you have to listen to me – you have no choice. But that's not always what happens. Raheem's performances should never have to be affected by stuff like this. We, as a team and as a club, are glad he played so well in this game and so many others, just like we were glad that David was able to perform under such difficult personal circumstances. Raheem should never have been put in a position where we all had to check that he was okay after being abused. It's ridiculous. This is a subject that's very important to me, and I feel it's therefore important to reflect on it here.

I also want to make it clear that I don't believe what happened to Raheem, and how he handled it, had any impact on the result of the game. We lost it and had to bounce back immediately as it was now obvious that in the Premier League title race Liverpool were a real force.

Champions League Group Game (6)
Wednesday 12 December
Etihad Stadium
Attendance: 50,411

MANCHESTER CITY	**2**
Sane (45, 61)	

HOFFENHEIM	**1**
Kramaric (16)	

City: Ederson, John Stones, Nicolas Otamendi, Aymeric Laporte, Oleksandr Zinchenko, Ilkay Gundogan, Phil Foden, Bernardo Silva, Gabriel Jesus, Raheem Sterling, Leroy Sane

Subs used: Kyle Walker, Fabian Delph, Vincent Kompany

Unused subs: Arijanet Muric, Riyad Mahrez, Brahim Diaz, Felix Nmecha

Booked: None

I made an appearance from the bench during this game as we completed our fixtures in the Champions League group stage. Leroy Sane scored both goals, after the German side had taken the lead to give us that kick we needed to really get going. After the Chelsea game, it was sad that this time it was Leroy who was on the end of some abuse, but he responded in the right way.

This was my first season at City where I thought the Champions League would slightly go ahead of the Premier League in our priorities. As much as you want to win this competition, you certainly don't want to give the Premier League away to anyone. You still want it to be yours. With Liverpool being so good and always so close throughout the season, there was never a moment when we could relax. Had we been leading the table by the sort of margin we managed the previous year, we could have given the Champions League special focus, but for us every game needed special focus. We had the same desire to win both competitions.

This game also provided another chance for Phil Foden to shine. We only needed a point to top the group, but Phil started the game and was only denied a goal by the brilliance of Baumann, who tipped over his impressive volley. We won the game and, along with the three other English clubs in the competition, progressed to the next stage. By topping our group we expected, in theory, to have a more favourable draw in the last sixteen, but there were some strong sides who had qualified in second place so we knew it would get harder from now as the draw would pit us against one of Ajax, Atletico Madrid, Roma or Schalke.

Premier League (17)
Saturday 15 December
Etihad Stadium
Attendance: 54,173

MANCHESTER CITY	3

Jesus (22, 50), Sterling (69)

EVERTON	1

Calvert-Lewin (65)

City: Ederson, Kyle Walker, Nicolas Otamendi, Aymeric Laporte, Fabian Delph, Fernandinho, Ilkay Gundogan, Bernardo Silva, Riyad Mahrez, Gabriel Jesus, Leroy Sane

Subs used: Raheem Sterling, Kevin de Bruyne

Unused subs: Arijanet Muric, John Stones, Oleksandr Zinchenko, Phil Foden, Sergio Aguero

Booked: Delph

Despite the defeat at Chelsea in our previous Premier League game, I didn't get my chance to return to the side in the next one against Everton. It was an important 3–1 win, which included a couple of goals from Gabriel Jesus and a lovely run and cross by Fernandinho to set up Raheem for the third. Gabriel is one of the young players I have the highest admiration for. You can admire people for many reasons; sometimes it's work rate, sometimes it's talent. But there's something else about him that makes him special in my eyes.

I've never known a kid – who's come from such a huge football market as Brazil, who's the number nine in the national team, and who's the real deal as a player – be so humble. He's so willing to learn and work hard. That sort of thing doesn't usually apply to a player with his background. It's definitely unusual. Let's face it, he's a super talent coming from a big country. He arrived with millions of pounds in endorsement deals and (typically of football these days) an inflated price tag and everything that goes with it. Usually with all that baggage you might expect him to think that he's already the finished article and that he'd be less willing to listen and learn. He's the opposite.

He came to City with the full commercial package, there's no doubt about that, but behind that façade there is a humble, hard-working, very clever young player with a big personality. He's a person who looks you in the eye every day and says 'good morning' and really means it when he asks you how you are. That's very, very rare. I haven't come across anyone else, in his position and with his stature, like this – ever.

The other thing that defines him is that he's had to compete for a place in the team with one of the best strikers in Kun Aguero that the Premier League has ever seen. He's taken that challenge, and everything else he's had to face, in his stride. He's willing to go toe to toe to compete for his place, to get an edge and to make himself better. I hope that he will be the successor one day. He deserves that so much. I don't know what will make that happen, but I just hope that at some stage he'll be in the same position Aguero is now.

Whenever Sergio wasn't playing throughout this season, Gabriel stepped in. We won so much during the season and Gabriel played a lot of games, so you can see that he was shining whenever he got the chance. His goal ratio was ridiculous. He started eight Premier League games, making twenty-one appearances from the bench, and scored seven goals. In the cups, he started thirteen games, and scored fourteen times. You can't beat players with energy and positive attitude and he's one of those people. He's got plenty of those attributes as well as amazing talent.

I believe it's only a matter of time before he's a player upon whom you can totally rely to score thirty goals a season. He'll eventually be the main man, all season, with someone else coming in and supporting him. I think he's very close to achieving that level, but he's probably still got one more step to make and that will be the biggest challenge for him during the next twenty-four months. I'm certain he's capable of getting there.

Having those options was something we felt gave us the slight edge over our rivals. By the end of November, Liverpool had been almost knocked out of the Champions League in the group stage, let's not forget, and they were showing signs of weakness when they rotated the squad. They could afford to change one or two positions, but they couldn't afford to change the whole team like we were doing. That led me to believe that eventually they would pick up injuries or something like that, and we'd be able to take advantage. The way I looked at it, they only had to drop three points, sometime somewhere, and then mentally they would be affected, which in turn would mean we'd come blasting through again, because we had that belief.

I was really amazed, though, that they seemed to have found a formula to keep on winning. Everyone knew what they were doing. Their tactics were far more predictable than ours, whereas with us it could be different from match to match. We were so much more flexible. We constantly changed our team and we were cute in what we were doing. They just overpowered everyone and I realised, *We've got to be careful here.* When Virgil van Dijk came in and sorted out the back line I thought, *Okay, it's game time now.* Now I really knew it.

Just occasionally there were slip-ups – but they were very rare. For example, when I saw their match at Wolves in the FA Cup in January, I knew they were going to lose that one, it seemed so obvious. It was just those little swaps of position and they didn't have the same intensity. Their game plan in that situation didn't work. When they had full intensity, with 100 per cent pressing, it was different. The way they were drilled and trained, and the way they were doing it, was just ruthless.

In retrospect, people might claim that we'd had it easy, but they forget that we actually had quite a lot of misfortune throughout the season. We certainly didn't have everything going for us. We had Riyad Mahrez missing the penalty at Anfield, that 'handball' against Wolves – a succession of events. Liverpool, on the other hand, had that ball that went along the top of the crossbar against Everton in their derby game and so on. There just seemed a series of those types of incidents that broke in their favour and even a few refereeing decisions that seemed to play a part.

This game came in the middle of that very hectic period of the season when the Champions League qualifiers are ending and the Carabao Cup is reaching the latter stages, so this win against Everton should not be undervalued. At one stage, Everton had pulled it back to 2–1 so one mistake and we could have dropped points. After the previous week's Premier League defeat at Chelsea, there could be no room for error in this one. We achieved our goal and we all knew that the next game was just three days away, so for those that played it was time to recover and for those that didn't it was time to focus on the next game.

Carabao Cup Quarter-Final
Tuesday 18 December
King Power Stadium
Attendance: 24,644

LEICESTER CITY   **1**
Albrighton (73)

MANCHESTER CITY   **1**
De Bruyne (14)

CITY WON 3–1 ON PENALTIES

City: Arijanet Muric, Kyle Walker, Eric Garcia, Nicolas Otamendi, Oleksandr Zinchenko, John Stones, Kevin de Bruyne, Phil Foden, Riyad Mahrez, Sergio Aguero, Brahim Diaz

Subs used: Raheem Sterling, Ilkay Gundogan, Gabriel Jesus

Unused subs: Ederson, Philippe Sandler, Fabian Delph, Felix Nmecha

Booked: Foden, Gundogan

Competition for places at City had never been more fierce and as we've seen there were usually three of us competing to play alongside Aymeric Laporte. In this game Pep chose another option as 17-year-old Eric Garcia got the chance to show his abilities. He'd played on the pre-season trip to the USA and is a potential star of the future. This was his debut in central defence, and he helped earn us a place in the semi-finals of the Carabao Cup via a penalty shoot-out.

Kevin de Bruyne was back in the starting line-up and scored with a wonderful shot from the edge of their penalty area on a wet night in the East Midlands to set us on our way. It wasn't until relatively late in the tie that Albrighton levelled things for Leicester. During the game, Aro Muric had made one brilliant full-length save, but it was during the penalty shoot-out that eventually decided the outcome of the game that he really proved to be the City hero that night. First, he saved James Maddison's spot kick low down to his right and then he kept out Caglar Soyuncu's effort low to his left. When Oleksandr Zinchenko calmly dispatched his attempt, we were through to the semi-final 3–1 on penalties.

The fixture was played right in the middle of the busy December period and was our fourth successive midweek game. We were glad to find a way past Leicester and keep going on all fronts. Although most people regard the Carabao Cup as the least important of the domestic trophies, as far as we were concerned we knew a win would leave us just one game away from a Wembley final. No team had ever won the treble of Premier League, FA Cup and League Cup and we certainly were not going to throw away the chance to achieve that by not taking this competition seriously.

Premier League (18)
Saturday 22 December
Etihad Stadium
Attendance: 53,340

MANCHESTER CITY	**2**

Gundogan (27), De Bruyne (85)

CRYSTAL PALACE	**3**

Schlupp (33), Townsend (35), Milivojevic (51)

City: Ederson, Kyle Walker, Nicolas Otamendi, Aymeric Laporte, Fabian Delph, John Stones, Bernardo Silva, Ilkay Gundogan, Raheem Sterling, Gabriel Jesus, Leroy Sane

Subs used: Sergio Aguero, Kevin de Bruyne, Riyad Mahrez

Unused subs: Arijanet Muric, Danilo, Oleksandr Zinchenko, Phil Foden

Booked: None

By losing at home to Crystal Palace, we allowed Liverpool to go four points clear in the title race. It was an unexpected defeat at home and a shock to the system. We'd taken the lead and were dominating possession, so there had been nothing to suggest that this game would end with defeat for us. One City fan described our performance as 'terrible' on Ian Cheeseman's *Forever Blue* YouTube vlog and moaned about us having no shots on target in the second half. I can understand why fans react like that – I'm a City fan myself – but there were others who argued that being just four points behind Liverpool as we neared the halfway mark of the season was not a gap that couldn't be closed. The truth was that we'd handed the initiative to Liverpool. They'd beaten Wolves the night before and were showing a consistency that none of us had expected. They hadn't lost a game and were almost halfway through the season, so a four-point advantage felt quite significant as it seemed clear that neither of us was going to drop many points.

All seemed to be going well when we took the lead through Ilkay Gundogan's header, before which we'd had several other chances to score. Then Jeffrey Schlupp equalised after John Stones had dispossessed one of the Palace players. Almost immediately after, Andros Townsend hit a wonder goal to give them the lead, with a magnificent first-time volley from outside the box. He couldn't have hit it better and sometimes you just have to acknowledge a goal of such quality. I can tell you, from personal experience, that those type of goals happen very infrequently. Finally, Luka Milivojevic scored a penalty, following a foul by Kyle Walker, to put them 3–1 up early in the second half. As we attempted get back into the game from 3–1 down, Gundo had a great shot wide and Leroy's free kick hit the post before Kevin eventually got one back.

As we got ready for Christmas, Liverpool seemed to have things going their way and we didn't. I felt they didn't deserve to win some of their games, and yet they usually managed to do so, whereas we had now lost a couple of games and hadn't had any lucky breaks. Every now and again you need a bit of luck.

Premier League (19)
Wednesday 26 December
King Power Stadium
Attendance: 32,090

LEICESTER CITY	**2**

Albrighton (19), Pereira (81)

MANCHESTER CITY	**1**

Bernardo Silva (14)

City: Ederson, Danilo, John Stones, Aymeric Laporte, Fabian Delph, Ilkay Gundogan, Kevin de Bruyne, Bernardo Silva, Raheem Sterling, Sergio Aguero, Leroy Sane

Subs used: David Silva, Riyad Mahrez

Unused subs: Arijanet Muric, Kyle Walker, Nicolas Otamendi, Oleksandr Zinchenko, Phil Foden

Booked: Stones, Aguero

Red card: Delph

Fans in particular always look forward to the traditional Boxing Day fixture, and after our previous defeat we were hoping to bring some Christmas cheer to them – but it didn't work out that way. We lost this game 2–1 at Leicester, which allowed Liverpool to open up a seven-point advantage at the top at the halfway point of the season. They'd dropped only six points so far and hadn't lost a Premier League game.

During the previous ten seasons, eight of the ten who'd topped the table at Christmas had gone on to win it. The two exceptions were Liverpool in 2008–09 when United had overtaken them, and Liverpool in 2013–14 when we caught and passed them. This season, we would have to do that again! To further complicate matters, Tottenham had also overtaken us.

With two defeats on the run and three in four, I was beginning to think we were swimming against the current, but I always had a deep-down belief we could catch them because we still had to play Liverpool at home. I felt that game against our biggest rivals would be a turning point. Until then, my aim was just to stay in touching distance.

To make matters worse, Fabian Delph was sent off in this game. He'd played at left back, like he had so many times during the Centurions season. A lot of people underestimate Fabian. They think he's this guy who's useful and can play in any position, help out and do a job for the team. They forget that he was the best left back in the league, by a country mile, during the Centurions season. The thing with Delphy is that he was always one of the most influential players in the dressing room.

He was a strong voice. He was always one of those people who put the team first and himself second. He's got a big personality so he has no issues with fronting people up if he thinks they're hiding or doing something that is to the detriment of the team. Guys like Delphy are the ones you want in your dressing room.

The club might buy a player because he's a left back or a midfielder and they'll play this way or that way, but in his case you were also buying a player that will hold other players in the team accountable. He was one of those who drove and pushed the dressing room to always want to strive to be better. He had a tough time throughout the treble season. In comparison to the level he had produced throughout the Centurions season, also a World Cup year, he was below the very high standards he had set for himself. There's no one more honest than him in that situation. He knew it himself.

Throughout last season, even though he made only thirteen starts, he still had a big influence on how the group was able to push on to a higher level every day. He brought a bit of bite into the team whenever he played. People might have forgotten that, particularly in the Mancini era, that was our strength. It was because of people like Delphy behind the scenes that we were very strong in that way. Zaba was like that, too.

In this game, Bernardo had given us the lead to suggest we'd be back on the right path, but Leicester, managed by Claude Puel, had other ideas and, with the scores level and ten minutes to go, Ricardo Pereira thrashed in a shot to win the game. Fabian's red card came after that, so wasn't significant in the outcome of the game. But we knew we had to get things back on track very soon, before the gap became too large.

Premier League (20)
Sunday 30 December
St Mary's Stadium
Attendance: 31,381

SOUTHAMPTON   **1**
Hojbjerg (37)

MANCHESTER CITY   **3**
David Silva (10), Ward-Prowse o.g. (45),
Aguero (45)

City: Ederson, Danilo, Vincent Kompany, Aymeric Laporte, Oleksandr Zinchenko, Fernandinho, Bernardo Silva, David Silva, Riyad Mahrez, Sergio Aguero, Raheem Sterling

Subs used: Gabriel Jesus, Leroy Sane, Kyle Walker

Unused subs: Arijanet Muric, John Stones, Nicolas Otamendi, Phil Foden

Booked: Aguero, Kompany, Danilo

I was back in the starting XI for this game. I suppose my chance had come because of the previous two defeats and, while I hadn't wanted City to lose, I now had a chance to prove I deserved my place in the team. The trip to Southampton came at the end of a month where we played a lot of games. We knew that the next opponents we faced were Liverpool, but it was important to be fully focused on this one, especially after the defeats against Crystal Palace and Leicester.

Charlie Austin is always a threat when he plays against us, and Ederson showed both sides of his game at St Mary's, with a great save from one of Austin's headers but also with his always impressive footwork. I played alongside Aymeric in defence and, as usual, we had the confidence of knowing that Ederson was in goal behind us.

Ederson has made a big impression at City, especially as he had such big shoes to fill. I think the spectre of Joe Hart was still floating around the club, even though he'd been gone for a year by the time Ederson joined. I don't care what anybody says, Joe Hart was a wonderful player for us. Some people's opinion of Harty probably changed because of the circumstances of his England career or what happened to him when he went abroad. But I'd say that Harty was our best player during his last season with us. He consistently won us trophies and titles in exactly the same way that Aguero or David Silva did, even the same way I did. People forget about that because somehow his image got tarnished by all the England stuff in the Euros. He admitted himself that he'd made a mistake against Wales when Gareth Bale scored and that he'd failed to stop Sigthorsson's winner against Iceland. As a goalkeeper every error is highlighted. We all make mistakes, but it seemed unfair to me that Joe's reputation was damaged, in the eyes of some people, by a couple of high-profile mistakes.

In terms of shot-stopping, Ederson had such great gloves to fill. In terms of the boots, Ederson, just like Claudio Bravo, brought something different to the team. Claudio was also the absolute master of playing out from the back. I've never seen anything like him, he's ridiculous, he's like a quarterback. Ederson provided the best of both worlds, the great shot-stopping of Harty and the great feet of Claudio, and he turned out to be the complete goalkeeper. I think Claudio is the whole package too, but I think he was just unlucky to have a first season where he had to handle every unfortunate thing the Premier League can throw at you.

For Ederson to come in and do what he did was amazing. I remember looking at film of him when he was at Benfica, but I couldn't find any clips of him making saves. Can you imagine looking for footage of a goalkeeper and you not finding any examples of saves, just his footwork? How times have changed. Even during his first few training sessions at the club, I don't think he put his gloves on for a week or so. I was watching this and thinking, *I've never seen this before*. As soon as he was in goal, though, I could see what powerful hands he had, and a commanding jump. He's got a huge presence on the pitch and in and around his goal. He's got a big personality and he's so cool and so calm.

One of the things Pep encouraged the keeper and the defenders to do was to play out from the back. To some, it seems a risky approach, as if you lose the ball so close to goal there's every chance the opposition might score. But thinking about it, now that I can fully reflect on my time at City, I can't remember a time we conceded a goal when we've been passing the ball around at the back. In three seasons, building up from our six-yard box, I can't recall one goal where the opposition have dispossessed us and then scored a goal. Even at Southampton away, where we played across the six-yard box with players pressing from every side, we got out.

When Claudio was playing, it was great as a defender to know that you could involve the keeper in these passing movements at the back. You could run as fast as you could into your position, and be confident that half the job was done. You knew that either of them would pick the right pass. When that's done it becomes a process that we'd practised day in day out. The next phase of playing out from the back is that you know how your opponents are going to press and what they're trying to achieve and of course we know when not to take the risk.

For that all to work smoothly, you need the main guy at the back to make the right calls. Ederson and Claudio were both superb at doing that. They're both incredibly cool. I think Ederson might be on a pulse rate of nineteen beats per minute while Claudio is twenty, but they're pretty similar in that respect.

Ederson is young, powerful and his progression as a player is so much greater than anyone else. You look back through your career for keepers that you felt safe with and I've got to be honest here, as much as Claudio had a tough first season, I'm a big admirer of his too. Playing from the back is such a big part of what we do, I still think he's a wonderful goalkeeper. The role that Ederson and Claudio played gives you such a sense of comfort at the back.

Claudio is incredibly well respected by everybody in the team. Maybe keepers are judged more on their physical presence in England, where I think it's seen as a little bit more important than in other leagues, I don't know. I'm just speculating, but perhaps for that reason Ederson has that bit more respect than Claudio. We don't know when Ederson's best time will be, but as he's still young it's probably not yet, when he's already incredible. That's why, for me, he'll just edge anyone in the end.

As the travelling City fans sang, 'We fight 'til the end, we're Man City we fight 'til the end,' we got back to winning ways, thanks to everyone. Liverpool were on a high; they'd beaten Arsenal at Anfield the day before our game on the south coast, but we reacted strongly to show that we would indeed fight to the end. As the new year dawned, we knew that nothing else would be enough if we were going to make 2019 as special as 2018 had been.

CHAPTER 6

JANUARY 2019

Premier League (21)
Thursday 3 January
Etihad Stadium
Attendance: 54,511

MANCHESTER CITY	2
Aguero (40), Sane (72)	
LIVERPOOL	1
Firmino (64)	

City: Ederson, Danilo, John Stones, Vincent Kompany, Aymeric Laporte, Fernandinho, Bernardo Silva, David Silva, Raheem Sterling, Sergio Aguero, Leroy Sane

Subs used: Ilkay Gundogan, Kyle Walker, Nicolas Otamendi

Unused subs: Arijanet Muric, Kevin de Bruyne, Riyad Mahrez, Gabriel Jesus

Booked: Ederson, Laporte, Bernardo Silva, Kompany

We simply had to win this game. We knew exactly what we had to do. Even a draw wouldn't have been a good result. It never mattered who we were facing, I always felt confident that we would win. I was sure we would eventually catch Liverpool, because I thought they would drop points against those same teams we had. That said, as far as this game was concerned, I believe if we'd lost this one the title race would have been over. If they had beaten us at the Etihad Stadium that night, it would have given them both momentum and a ten-point leeway. It would also have had a big effect on us psychologically, and things don't normally go right after that. Losing at your own stadium against your title rivals wouldn't be a good thing.

I know the City fans were singing 'Campeones, Campeones' after that win, but I think that was just a bit of banter aimed at the Liverpool fans, rather than them assuming we were going to beat them in the title race. There were still seventeen games to go, and both sides would surely drop points along the way. The City fans were very loud too, they were obviously up for it like we were and were roaring all the way through. I don't know if that came from wanting revenge for the defeats we'd suffered against them the previous season and the bus incident or whether they could sense that we were fighting again, with our backs against the wall.

I think that was highest intensity match of my career. I played in central defence, of course, but John Stones and Aymeric Laporte also started, and every player involved was completely focused on achieving what we needed to. The whole squad turned up with an incredible desire to win, plus there were nearly 55,000 other people involved in the game, pushing you on to a win.

That atmosphere, that feeling, gives you an extra 10 or 20 per cent more and it was ignited with the challenge by Fernandinho early on, when he absolutely crashed into one of their players. He came out of it on top and set up a counter-attack. That was unbelievable. Bernardo Silva followed it up in similar style and there was a level of aggression in the side that we brought out at the right time. I think that was one of our strengths as a team. We showed the same personality in the home game against Tottenham in the Champions League. I think that's when we were at our best.

City fans do seem to like a losing position for some reason, that's when they get ready for the game and go, *Here we go, 3–0 down, no problem, here we go, that's what we like!* I'm not saying that being 3–0 down was a common position for City to be in, but it's just a feeling City fans have when their backs are against the wall.

The intensity was so high in that game that if the crowd sang 'Here's to you, Vincent Kompany' I wouldn't have noticed. We had no time to focus on anything else but what was happening on the pitch. There were runs going on everywhere; every pass you make in games like that is under pressure, every tackle you make is against someone who is really good. We were on our toes every time they got near our box, and it felt like there were 8,000 Liverpool fans getting louder when that happened.

You can imagine the noise levels and power of concentration in our minds when John Stones cleared that ball off the line, and the anxiety as we waited for confirmation that it hadn't fully crossed the line. They're edge-of-the-seat type of games. Those are the best. I always wanted to be part of those occasions. Tottenham at home in the Champions League was the same type of encounter.

Liverpool hit the post at 0–0 and then there was that Stones clearance off the line, when goal-line technology showed the ball had not crossed by millimetres. Talking of fine margins, Aguero's shot from a tight angle that gave us the lead was like threading the eye of a needle; there was only one place he could have hit that shot and he did.

Roberto Firmino got them level, but a brilliant counter-attacking goal by us saw Raheem send Leroy into a position where he could score into the bottom corner. Kun nearly added a third after that, only denied by their goalkeeper when he tried to go around him. Bernardo and Raheem also had chances to add further goals, but the main thing was that we won.

If ever the expression a 'six-pointer' was used correctly, then it was for this game. Pep said after the game that anything other than a win was not an option, 'I'm proud of them, but not just today. We lost two games in four days, but you can't forget what we have done for sixteen months. We knew that it was a final today, if we lose it is almost over. We were not scared, we had no fear. They are the [Premier League] leaders [by four points], but we have reduced the gap. We knew that if we won we would be in contention to fight for the Premier League. I don't remember a league so tough, there are so many huge contenders fighting for the title. Every game is a final.'

FA Cup Third Round
Sunday 6 January
Etihad Stadium
Attendance: 52,708

MANCHESTER CITY   **7**
Sterling (12), Foden (43), Ajayi o.g. (45), Jesus
(52), Mahrez (73), Otamendi (78), Sane (85)

ROTHERHAM   **0**

City: Ederson, Kyle Walker, John Stones, Nicolas Otamendi, Oleksandr Zinchenko, Ilkay Gundogan, Phil Foden, Kevin de Bruyne, Raheem Sterling, Riyad Mahrez, Gabriel Jesus

Subs used: Leroy Sane, Philippe Sandler, Danilo

Unused subs: Arijanet Muric, Aymeric Laporte, Bernardo Silva, Fernandinho

Booked: Sterling

This game was the start of a few weeks on the sidelines for me as I dealt with my latest injury setback, but it was also during a period when the attacking side of our team was really able to show what they could do. These matches against lower-division opposition might seem a foregone conclusion, but teams like Rotherham play as well as they can and there's always a real danger that if you don't get things absolutely right in your team, you come unstuck.

We scored seven goals in this game, and just a few days later it was an even bigger winning margin against Burton. I've heard the suggestion that winning by such big margins is disrespectful to the other team. No way. You should always go for more and more and more. I believe that playing as well as you can and scoring as many goals as you can is a sign of respect to your opponents. I really believe that. The other thing I always think, when I look at it from a player's perspective, is that your career is way too short to start easing off on anything. Every player should go hard, do the best you can in every game you play. If the final score is 20–0 then so be it.

The moment you give an inch on the pitch is the moment you start to unravel and go into decline. The great thing about playing in all these cup competitions and progressing to the later stages is that there are plenty of games for all the members of our squad. Gabriel Jesus played in this one, alongside Phil Foden, and every minute on the pitch is precious when you play in a great team like ours.

Phil scored a goal too, so it would have been another boost of confidence for him. I certainly see all the English cup competitions as very important and don't view the number of games the teams play by progressing in the FA Cup or Carabao Cup as a problem. Everyone wants to play, everyone wants to win and there is a fantastic competition for places. We won this game, so we were off and running in the FA Cup, which we'd last won back in 2011 and we all wanted to win it again.

Carabao Cup Semi-Final (First Leg)
Wednesday 9 January
Etihad Stadium
Attendance: 32,089

MANCHESTER CITY   **9**
De Bruyne (5), Jesus (30, 34, 57, 65),
Zinchenko (37), Foden (62), Walker (70),
Mahrez (83)

BURTON ALBION   **0**

City: Arijanet Muric, Kyle Walker, Nicolas Otamendi, Eric Garcia, Oleksandr Zinchenko, Kevin de Bruyne, Ilkay Gundogan, David Silva, Riyad Mahrez, Gabriel Jesus, Leroy Sane

Subs used: Phil Foden, Bernardo Silva, Danilo

Unused subs: Ederson, John Stones, Fabian Delph, Raheem Sterling

Booked: None

Pep had promised to take every competition we played in as seriously as the other. He selected a very strong team, or at least that's the way others perceived it, but as far as I was concerned our squad was so strong that whoever had been selected was top quality. Eric Garcia played in defence alongside Nico, but it was the attacking side of our football that made the headlines.

We'd put seven goals past Rotherham in the FA Cup and now nine past Burton in the Carabao Cup. These games had followed the vital win against Liverpool in the Premier League; the momentum that we'd lost with defeats to Palace and Leicester was now fully restored and we were still in almost perfect positions in all three domestic trophies.

For Gabriel to score four goals in a match, in fact for anyone to score so many in one game, is something to be proud of regardless of the opposition. The fact that we were 4–0 up before half-time effectively meant that the tie was already over, even though our professionalism would never allow us to think that way. Eighteen goals scored in less than a week was certainly a huge confidence booster to all of us, especially as the vital win against Liverpool was part of those seven days.

The last time City won by a nine-goal margin was back on 7 November 1987, when David White, Paul Stewart and Tony Adcock each scored hat-tricks. It was becoming a season of breaking records or equalling records, but winning trophies was our priority, and even the emphatic win against Burton did not mean that the second leg would be treated as a formality. Effectively, though, we were booked in for our first cup final of the season.

Premier League (22)
Monday 14 January
Etihad Stadium
Attendance: 54,171

MANCHESTER CITY   **3**
Jesus (10, 39), Coady o.g. (78)

WOLVERHAMPTON WANDERERS   **0**

City: Ederson, Kyle Walker, John Stones, Aymeric Laporte, Danilo, Fernandinho, Bernardo Silva, David Silva, Raheem Sterling, Gabriel Jesus, Leroy Sane

Subs used: Kevin de Bruyne, Ilkay Gundogan, Sergio Aguero

Unused subs: Arijanet Muric, Nicolas Otamendi, Fabian Delph, Riyad Mahrez

Booked: Fernandinho

Finally, after a break of eleven days since our last Premier League game, we could continue the chase. This match was another one where we dominated possession. We won the game fairly comfortably in the end, but it was the third of a sequence of games that I missed through injury.

Let me clear up my injury situation once and for all. I'll start at the beginning. My biggest issue was that early in my career I started having surgeries, for one-off reasons after a variety of different incidents.

When you've got to go under the knife, you just have to accept it. But every time it happens, scar tissue starts to build up and your biomechanics change a little bit. On top of that, when you start having muscle pulls, you accumulate even more scar tissue. Whether it's on your skin or buried out of sight in the muscle itself, it can make everything around it less mobile and pliable. The less mobility you have in your calf or hamstring or whatever it is that's affected, the more likely you are to have pulls at some point in the future. It becomes a vicious circle and that's a natural consequence of the changes your body goes through. In my case, I've always had a natural tendency to ignore the warning signs and push myself through every barrier that's put in front of me.

I've played with broken bones, muscles half torn or on the edge of pulling, but I got away with it when I was younger. However, there's a cost. When you carry on playing with something that's not quite right, you also prevent it from healing properly. Eventually it ends up being twice as bad as it would have been if you'd stopped and allowed it to heal. I had a side of me that always wanted to show that I was one of the strongest and that I was always going to be invincible. This probably explains why so many things started to go wrong for me, injury-wise, later in my career. It's logical when you think about it.

The reason I've continued to fight back from all these injury problems is because I'm an eternal optimist. I always visualise the one possibility that could happen, like scoring from 30 yards during the last game of the season or rising to win an important header to beat United in a vital derby on the way to winning the title, or making a match-winning tackle. In my mind, that makes everything I have had to go through irrelevant because the outcome is worth every second of pain along the way. I have always believed those moments would happen for me.

From the time I go for surgery to the instant I achieve those great moments on the field, that optimism is always in my mind. Perhaps that's where I'm a little different to some players. I won't allow myself to give up or stop believing. I kept coming back and hitting those objectives at the right time. It's because I've always believed in myself from the first minute to the very last second when those pivotal, significant moments in your career happen.

Another factor during the latter part of my time at City was that I had gained a lot of experience and knowledge about my body, so I wasn't trying to prove anything to anyone any more. I have a lot of gratitude towards Pep because he gave me the confidence during his time at the club to not have to always play at my maximum or prove anything in training. If he wanted me to play, then I would always be ready, but, if Pep didn't select me, he didn't make me feel I needed to push myself further in training. I always knew that he was confident that if he did select me, I'd be as good as I'd ever been. That took a lot of weight off my shoulders. I didn't have to be the most macho in training, the warrior or an animal every time I was on the training field. I could save it for the right moments. That benefited my health.

There might be people who think that what I'm describing is a bit like Ledley King's situation in his final years at Tottenham. He didn't train as much as his teammates during the week because of his injury problems. He tried to manage himself through each week, but my circumstances were different. He had cartilage damage, a chronic issue. That's never been my case. If you go back through the history of my problems, they've almost always been muscle injuries. It's simply been a case of muscle breaks down and then the muscle repairs. The cycle just repeats itself and that's really all there is to it.

Every now and again I would go for surgery and I'd start my recovery until the next problem occured. One of the worst issues I had was when I pulled my rec fem (rectus femoris, the quadricep muscles at the front of my thigh) at Real Madrid in the Champions League semi-final and

I was out for four months and had to have surgery. If that had been a chronic injury, I would have developed issues by now.

I've been very, very fortunate not to have had any long-term problems associated with any of my injuries, whether it be when I had problems with my Achilles tendon, my shoulder or anything else. They were all very different injuries. In terms of athleticism and mobility, I'm actually very good. If I'd had those big cartilage injuries, I couldn't have got over them in some superhuman way, I would have been like everyone else. At some point I would have been finished off with those kind of issues.

The biggest weakness of my condition is that when I don't play consistently, it can happen over and over again. The normal pattern is that you break down more. A muscle is like anything. You've got to train it and make it resistant to loading; when you come back from injuries it's always the most difficult period of recovery. The beginning of the return to training or playing is when you're most likely to see the injury recur.

When you are often in that phase, the hardest thing for you to do is to trust your body to play and to go right to your limit without breaking down again. Usually you know that after you've played four or five games you're back into full stride again and you have confidence in what your body can do. Even your healthy body has scars here and there, but once you're in decline, you're in decline.

As an athlete you are genetically sound; you must be or you wouldn't have been able to perform in the first place. The only issue that you have when you play for a club like City is that you don't always get four or five games to get back your full match fitness. I needed to be ready every minute of every game. I didn't lose a game playing for City during my final eighteen months, but I always felt pressure to be at my very best in every game I played. Rightly or wrongly, I worried that I was one bad performance away from my first-team chances being reduced to a minimum.

That's the pressure you're dealing with now at City. Every time I came back from injury, I knew that this could be my last game. The wheel of change is powerful. You can't stop it. You might be able to slow it down a bit, every now and again, but you can't stop it. It took everything I had to keep it at bay, just so that I felt I had a little bit of control over my own destiny. That's why I decided when I did to get out from underneath that wheel. That was how I thought about my future at the club; I had no idea if Pep thought that way, or if he'd have been happy for me to carry on playing beyond this season.

As a result of how Wolves had played against us at Molineux earlier in the season, I knew this game would be another one we couldn't take for granted, as we all respected them so much. Fortunately for us, Willy Boly was sent off with just nineteen minutes on the clock after a bad tackle on Bernardo Silva, so this became a fairly straightforward win. Although the gap to Liverpool remained at four points, we were the top scorers in the Premier League with fifty-nine goals. All we had to do now was to keep the pressure on Liverpool and continue winning.

Premier League (23)
Sunday 20 January
John Smith's Stadium
Attendance: 24,190

HUDDERSFIELD TOWN	0
MANCHESTER CITY	3

Danilo (18), Sterling (54), Sane (56)

City: Ederson, Kyle Walker, Nicolas Otamendi, Aymeric Laporte, Danilo, Fernandinho, Kevin de Bruyne, Ilkay Gundogan, Raheem Sterling, Sergio Aguero, Leroy Sane

Subs used: David Silva, Bernardo Silva, Fabian Delph

Unused subs: Arijanet Muric, John Stones, Phil Foden, Gabriel Jesus

Booked: Walker, Fernandinho

On paper, this would be one of the easier games during our second half of the season. Huddersfield were bottom of the table and by the time we played this game everyone knew that their relegation had become inevitable. The danger was that we would take winning, even at their ground, for granted. We knew that there was no room for error and we'd already started to think that we might have to win every single game that was left to have a chance of over-hauling Liverpool and retaining our title.

The day before our trip to West Yorkshire, Liverpool

had played Crystal Palace at Anfield. They'd been behind, recovered to take the lead, and then been pegged back again. Those are the sort of games that can affect you psychologically if you lose them, but Liverpool found a way to win 4–3 in the end, so to emerge victorious in those circumstances was likely to have a very positive effect on their morale.

We simply had to win at Huddersfield to show that we were still very much in this title race. The home supporters were right behind their team, despite the position their club was in, but we scored three goals and showed that we were not going to give up. This was another game where the quality of Leroy Sane shone through in key moments. It was his pinpoint cross for Raheem Sterling that gave us a two-goal advantage and then his brilliant control followed by a calm and precise finish that gave us our third. Danilo's deflected shot that opened the scoring had been our 100th goal of the season, in all competitions.

Huddersfield had just parted company with their manager David Wagner, but sometimes those types of changes lead to a team trying even harder, so we knew we couldn't play at anything less than our very best. Pep wasn't gushing in his praise when he spoke to the BBC after the game. He said, 'The way we played we didn't deserve more than three goals. We will improve in the future. We always have to demand from ourselves to do the very best we can in every single game. They defended deep, aggressively and man to man and sometimes it's not easy to find the spaces. We have to win our games, we don't focus on what Liverpool does.'

⚽

Carabao Cup Semi-Final (Second Leg)
Wednesday 23 January
Pirelli Stadium
Attendance: 6,591

BURTON ALBION	**0**
MANCHESTER CITY	**1**

Aguero (26)

City: Arijanet Muric, Danilo, Eric Garcia, Philippe Sandler, Oleksandr Zinchenko, Kevin de Bruyne, Fabian Delph, Phil Foden, Riyad Mahrez, Sergio Aguero, Ian Carlo Poveda

Subs used: Gabriel Jesus, Benjamin Mendy, Felix Nmecha

Unused subs: Daniel Grimshaw, John Stones, Luke Bolton, Taylor Richards

Booked: None

I suppose that no one will be surprised if I say that we had no doubts we'd be travelling to Wembley for the Carabao Cup final before we even played this second leg. We still had to be respectful and focused to make sure something silly didn't happen at Burton. In the early days of my time at City, the fans would use the expression 'typical City' to explain how the club's history was full of incidents where the team would snatch defeat from the jaws of success.

Sergio Aguero and Kevin de Bruyne started the game at Burton, despite our 9–0 lead from the first leg, and we showed our lower-division opponents total respect by play-ing as well as we were allowed to play. If there had been criticism from some quarters about the margin of victory in the first leg, those same people might have suggested we should let them win the second leg. The match was played on a very difficult surface, which became harder as the game went along and the temperature dropped. We ended up win-ning 1–0 on the night, Kun scoring the winner. From my point of view, we were through to another Wembley final and, as always, I was determined to be fit by the time that game came around at the end of February so I could lead the side out.

FA Cup Fourth Round
Saturday 26 January
Etihad Stadium
Attendance: 50,121

MANCHESTER CITY   **5**
Jesus (23), Bernardo Silva (52), De Bruyne
(61), Long o.g. (73), Aguero (85)

BURNLEY   **0**

City: Ederson, Kyle Walker, John Stones, Nicolas Otamendi, Danilo, Fernandinho, Kevin de Bruyne, Ilkay Gundogan, Riyad Mahrez, Gabriel Jesus, Bernardo Silva

Up against a familiar foe in Samir Nasri. Our 1–0 victory over West Ham was one of five by that scoreline in eleven games during the title run-in.

Clearing the ball during our hard-fought 3–1 win over Watford in March.

After Liverpool won against Chelsea, we knew we had to beat Palace to maintain our one-point lead at the top of the table, with just five more games left to play after this one.

Fernando Llorente scored what would prove to be the winning goal in our Champions League quarter-final tie against Spurs. He didn't mean to, but I saw the ball hit his hand – and, according to the rules, it should not have been given.

I also had a good view of the other controversial VAR moment, when Raheem Sterling's late winner was ruled out because Aguero had been offside in the build-up.

People said that the pace of the United attack, featuring Marcus Rashford, would cause me problems, but, as I got older, I learned how to deal with speedy forwards, even if I wasn't quite as quick as I had been. We handled everything United could throw at us, and I knew we would have tougher challenges before the season was over.

'Don't shoot!' yelled Ilkay Gundogan, but I did and it proved to be the winner in our game against Leicester City – a vitally important moment in our run-in.

My family joined me on the pitch after I'd played my last game at the Etihad as a City player – we were two games away from winning every domestic trophy.

Celebrating with Riyad Mahrez after he'd scored the third goal against Brighton to ensure we would hold on to our title. Earlier in the season, when we were both on the bench, I had told him his moment would come.

It had been a relentless season, but finally we had won the Premier League, despite Liverpool having accumulated ninety-seven points to push us all the way.

Battling it out with Abdoulaye Doucoure of Watford during the FA Cup final. As the lead grew, I was able to enjoy my last game for the club.

I was proud to wear the red and black scarf, matching the colours of City's 1969 FA Cup-winning side, in memory of Bernard Halford, the former City secretary who died earlier in the year.

The parade through Manchester was a special moment, celebrating a unique domestic treble.

Saying my goodbyes and thank yous before it was time to drop the mic.

Thanks for everything.

Subs used: David Silva, Sergio Aguero, Phil Foden

Unused subs: Arijanet Muric, Aymeric Laporte, Raheem Sterling, Leroy Sane

Booked: Walker

I wasn't involved in the FA Cup game against Burnley, but it proved to be another straightforward win for us. Kevin de Bruyne played seventy-five minutes of the game as he continued to get back into his rhythm as he returned from injury. He was among the goalscorers, along with Bernardo Silva, who really shone in the match.

I think everyone looks at Bernardo as a top player. He's still so young, having only turned twenty-four years of age during this amazing season. I believe he's at the start of something very special for City. He's been at the club for two seasons and everything he has done so far has been tremendous. He's going to go from strength to strength. When you look at Bernardo, you can recognise all the signs of a future City legend, depending on whether he decides to stay for that long or not. It's all in his hands.

What makes him a special player, and not just a gifted player, is he's such a positive guy. It's very natural to him. I also call him a leader, I've told him that and he laughs at me when I say it. There are so many different types of leadership. His natural ability to be positive, all the time, and to influence the group by being like that, makes such a difference.

He'll come to training, or the dressing room, always ready for action. He trains at 100 per cent and he does it with a smile. It's infectious. That's a very important quality to have as a leader. When he's on the pitch, he's one of the most talented players and yet he always works as hard, if not harder, than anyone else. That's another side of leadership. He might laugh at me, but maybe that's the next step for him to realise what he needs to do to be in the highest category of leader one day.

Bernardo is an artist as well. His positive energy and personality turns into creativity when he is on the pitch. He's like a kid. He plays more football than anyone I know. He plays football in the dressing room. I'm not saying that senior pros lose that, but sometimes you start to look after your body in different ways which can mean you don't always get as much joy out of all the extra football you play. All the extra bits 'mess with your programme', but he doesn't care. His ability and creativity make him do stuff that not many people can do, if I'm being honest.

He's walking in the footsteps of some unbelievable players at the club, such as David Silva, Samir Nasri, in terms of the sort of player he is. If he can carry on like he was when I was playing alongside him at City, there's a chance for him to be on a par with the greats of this club.

Could he one day win the Ballon d'Or? Of course. He could achieve anything, but the problem for Bernardo is that he's so humble. He'll always drop a couple of places in the contenders' list just because of that. There will always be guys that are better at self-promotion and have better PR machines around them. I'd say his Ballon d'Or situation is the same as it is for every City player.

When you think about it there are a lot of City players who should have won it or deserve to win it in the future. If you think about what Kun Aguero has achieved already or David Silva or Kevin de Bruyne or one of our defenders, there are so many players who have the level of ability to win it, and deserve to. The problem at City is that we have to win the Champions League. There's no point in talking about the Ballon d'Or without winning the Champions League. That's the main thing, really. If you win the Champions League, you are 90 per cent of the way there.

Kevin was now starting to show the quality that would help us push on through the remaining games of the season, when we knew we would probably have to win every game remaining if we were to secure the four trophies we still had hopes of winning. The third goal of this tie was a typical razor-sharp shot from 25 yards out and he was involved in the own goal that made it four.

Sean Dyche, the Burnley manager, claimed we could 'win everything' after this victory. Pep summed up our overall position by saying, 'We've won one title [the Community Shield], we are in another one [Carabao Cup final] and we want to be in the last stages of the FA Cup, arrive in the right moment against Schalke [in the Champions League] and fight until the end in the Premier League.'

Premier League (24)
Tuesday 29 January
St James' Park
Attendance: 50,861

NEWCASTLE UNITED   **2**
Rondon (66), Ritchie (80)

MANCHESTER CITY   **1**
Aguero (1)

City: Ederson, Kyle Walker, John Stones, Aymeric Laporte, Danilo, Fernandinho, Kevin de Bruyne, David Silva, Raheem Sterling, Sergio Aguero, Leroy Sane

Subs used: Bernardo Silva, Gabriel Jesus

Unused subs: Arijanet Muric, Nicolas Otamendi, Ilkay Gundogan, Phil Foden, Riyad Mahrez

Booked: Laporte, Sterling, De Bruyne

This game couldn't have started any better for us with Raheem Sterling's cross headed back by David Silva for Kun to put us ahead after twenty-four seconds. I don't know how David was so aware of things around him as he stumbled and fell as the ball from Raheem headed towards him, and yet he managed to head the ball perfectly into Aguero's path. At that moment, with Liverpool playing Leicester the following night, we were just one point behind them in the title race. A few minutes later, Kevin de Bruyne had played a perfect free kick to Sergio, who turned it in at the near post only for the referee to book Kevin for taking it before he blew his whistle. That would have made it 2–0.

We dominated the game and could have added other goals but on sixty-six minutes Newcastle drew level, and suddenly the atmosphere in the ground changed. Fourteen minutes later, they took the lead from the penalty spot, after a foul by Fernandinho. With fourteen games to go, the defeat meant that if Liverpool won the following night they would be seven points ahead of us, which would have been a very large gap to make up when they were dropping so few points.

After the game, Pep did his best to keep our spirits up when he told the press, 'We are in January, there are a lot of games but of course when you are chasing the leader you can't afford to drop points. I love these players and all I will continue to do is to try to help them. I know how they feel right now. They are an incredible group of players. If Liverpool win tomorrow then they will be a lot of points ahead but this is January, not April or May.'

At that point, if I'm really honest, I think Pep started to play mind games with us – either that or he really didn't believe in us any more. I felt like a lot of the belief had gone at the club, and I think there were a lot of people who didn't still believe we could win the league. Almost everyone was stunned by this result.

I had nothing else to do, because I wasn't involved in that game, so I was in the right frame of mind to come in the next day and say to everyone, 'Come on guys, we can still do this. We can do this, they'll slip up.' I didn't know where it was going to come from, but I knew we could push through and win twenty games in a row if we had to. When we were in the right state of mind, I really didn't believe any team could beat us. To get into that frame of mind for such a long time was going to require a herculean effort. Maybe it was a 1 per cent chance, but I certainly wasn't going to give it up just yet.

I don't think anyone can top Churchill in the way he gave inspirational speeches, but I was just hoping that my rallying call could make a difference. I've done a few speeches over the years, usually in the bad moments, like after the defeat at Arsenal in the 2012 season. I often speak up in these moments when belief is low and everybody seems to have given up. I'm always the one naïve guy who stands up and says, 'Guys, you can still do it.' Nine times out of ten it doesn't happen, but it just takes one.

My thing is that hope always lifts you, sometimes you just have to reset the button and look at things from a new perspective. There are always little opportunities, little slip-ups by your opponents. I've been involved so many times in leagues and competitions where this has happened.

We'd played before Liverpool for once and had had the chance to narrow the gap before their game against Leicester, so when we came home empty-handed, it felt to many that the title race was over. I hoped my speech to the players the next day would keep them believing. And we immediately had some good fortune, as Liverpool drew 1–1 with Leicester the following night. They increased their lead to five points, but they hadn't won and made it seven, which kept our hopes up.

CHAPTER 7

FEBRUARY 2019

Premier League (25)
Sunday 3 February
Etihad Stadium
Attendance: 54,483

MANCHESTER CITY   **3**
Aguero (1, 44, 61)

ARSENAL   **1**
Koscielny (11)

City: Ederson, Kyle Walker, Nicolas Otamendi, Aymeric Laporte,
Fernandinho, Ilkay Gundogan, Kevin de Bruyne, Bernardo Silva, David
Silva, Raheem Sterling, Sergio Aguero

Subs used: Gabriel Jesus, Riyad Mahrez

Unused subs: Arijanet Muric, Danilo, John Stones, Fabian Delph, Leroy Sane

Booked: Gundogan

If my optimistic words made any difference we'll never know, but what was certain was that we had to win every single match from now on. Arsenal were our next opponents and the team were back to their best. Sergio Aguero scored a hat-trick and we had the first of the fourteen wins we needed from our remaining league games. Because they had played before us, we had dropped a point behind Tottenham ahead of the game, but the only thing we cared about was keeping the pressure on Liverpool and making sure we were ready to capitalise on any slip-ups that they made.

The first goal, just like at Newcastle, had come inside the first minute – this time we had to wait forty-six seconds before Kun headed home – but Arsenal drew level quite quickly, so there was still a lot more to do in this game before we could be sure of all three points. We carried on playing patiently, believing that the chances would come and, sure enough, Sergio added a second just before half-time, well set up by Raheem, before he completed his hat-trick by bundling the ball in with an hour gone. We were back to winning ways in the Premier League.

Pep's verdict was simple: 'I don't know when, or even if, Liverpool will slip up. Of course I can't deny that we hope that West Ham beats Liverpool [tomorrow], but I don't have influence over that game. Of course we have to win every game, especially after the defeat at Newcastle. We expected Liverpool to beat Leicester. A lot of things can happen between now and the end of the season. At every press conference I am asked if the pressure is on us, or is it on Liverpool, but I don't know, all I can do is to try to help my team to win every game. I would prefer to be in Liverpool's position in the title race. The pressure is tougher on us because if we drop points it will be even tougher. The important thing is to be ourselves.'

Liverpool drew 1–1 at West Ham the following day – one report said they were suffering from 'stage fright' because they hadn't won the league since 1990 – meaning that City were now just three points behind Liverpool with thirteen games to go. So, although we'd lost one of our previous two games, we'd actually managed to close the gap during that period. That was more important than who was coping with the pressure or not.

Premier League (26)
Wednesday 6 February
Goodison Park
Attendance: 39,322

| **EVERTON** | **0** |
| **MANCHESTER CITY** | **2** |

Laporte (45), Jesus (90)

City: Ederson, Kyle Walker, John Stones, Nicolas Otamendi, Aymeric Laporte, Fernandinho, Ilkay Gundogan, Bernardo Silva, David Silva, Sergio Aguero, Leroy Sane

Subs used: Raheem Sterling, Gabriel Jesus, Kevin de Bruyne

Unused subs: Arijanet Muric, Danilo, Oleksandr Zinchenko, Riyad Mahrez

Booked: Fernandinho

I wasn't in the team for this game, but what I do remember quite clearly is how many Evertonians contacted me at this time. Inside the stadium there was no doubt the home fans wanted their team to win, but when they realised we were the better team that night, they changed. They wanted us to win every game from that point on, so that their city rivals didn't claim the title. They were saying to me very bluntly, 'Do not lose.' Even though there has always been an intense Manc v Scouse rivalry, this was different. Clubs and their supporters have their own affiliations and histories and we've all heard that expression, the enemy of my enemy is my friend. That's probably the best way to sum it up.

During my years at City, games at Everton had never been easy and this was not going to be any different, despite some fans saying beforehand that this was one game they wouldn't be too upset to lose. It was a tough game and we weren't always at our best, but neither did we seem under too much pressure. Aymeric scored from a free kick by David Silva at the end of the first half, and then Gabriel finished off a goal set up by fellow substitute Kevin de

Bruyne right at the end of the match. That win took us above Liverpool on goal difference. It was the first time we'd been top of the Premier League since 15 December, even though we knew Liverpool would play their game in hand on Saturday, before our game against Chelsea. We were top, though, for now at least, and that was important, especially as a few days earlier we could have been seven points behind.

Pep acknowledged that the squad had not given up, despite the impression I might have had from him after the Newcastle game, and that he knew we were incredibly motivated and he'd never questioned us.

Premier League (27)
Sunday 10 February
Etihad Stadium
Attendance: 54,452

MANCHESTER CITY	**6**

Sterling (4, 80), Aguero (13, 19, 56),
Gundogan (25)

CHELSEA	**0**

City: Ederson, Kyle Walker, John Stones, Aymeric Laporte, Oleksandr Zinchenko, Fernandinho, Kevin de Bruyne, Ilkay Gundogan, Bernardo Silva, Raheem Sterling, Sergio Aguero

Subs used: Gabriel Jesus, Riyad Mahrez, David Silva

Unused subs: Arijanet Muric, Danilo, Nicolas Otamendi, Leroy Sane

Booked: Gundogan

Pep wanted the team to return to the fearless attacking football that we knew we were capable of for this one – and he got his wish. A 6–0 home win against Chelsea gave everyone a huge boost. By now, the intense competition with the other teams at the top of the table had lifted our performance to a new level. We were all fully focused and believing again, and I'm sure that a performance like this, against such high-quality opposition, would send a clear message that we intended winning all our remaining games, which in turn meant that Liverpool couldn't afford any more dropped points.

This was almost a perfect performance, with us going 4–0 up in the first twenty-five minutes, and it featured another Sergio Aguero hat-trick. After the game he said, 'I think this was one of the best performances of the team. I missed a chance when really I should have scored, early in the game, but then I just carried on trying to think how I could help the team and score goals, and during the next few minutes I was able to score a really good goal with a shot from far out into the top corner. I've scored fifteen City hat-tricks and I'm happy to break records for the club, but what really matters in the end is winning.'

Pep described it as one of the best home performances he'd seen as City manager. He said, 'It has been a good week with this win against Chelsea and also at Everton.

Finally, now we can have two days off before we start to prepare for Newport. A week ago we lost to Newcastle; this is football.'

It felt like this was a big statement in the title race, but it also took us all a bit by surprise. We were lethal that day, clinical and sharp. It was an all-round exceptional performance. It was beautiful to witness, even from the sidelines. It was nice to sit back and watch that game knowing that we were all part of something special. At Stamford Bridge earlier in the season they'd made it very hard for us, though we eventually won the game 2–0. The only concern was that this 6–0 win had happened just two weeks before we were to play them again in the Carabao Cup final. We knew, from the moment we won this game so emphatically, that the game at Wembley would be much harder as a result.

FA Cup Fifth Round
Saturday 16 February
Rodney Parade
Attendance: 9,680

NEWPORT COUNTY   **1**
Amond (88)

MANCHESTER CITY   **4**
Sane (51), Foden (75, 89), Mahrez (90)

City: Ederson, Danilo, John Stones, Nicolas Otamendi, Oleksandr Zinchenko, Fernandinho, Phil Foden, David Silva, Riyad Mahrez, Gabriel Jesus, Leroy Sane

Subs used: Aymeric Laporte, Ilkay Gundogan

Unused subs: Arijanet Muric, Kyle Walker, Kevin de Bruyne, Raheem Sterling, Bernardo Silva

Booked: None

The Newport manager, Michael Flynn, said before the game that if his side were to beat us in this game it would be the greatest Cup upset of all time. I'm not sure I agree with him, but that statement makes you realise what a big game it was for Newport and their supporters. Flynn was introduced to Pep before the game and was quoted as saying, 'It's a pleasure to see you, you're an absolute genius.'

It was hard work in South Wales, and late on Newport got things back to 2–1, but a second goal from Phil Foden – a great left-footed finish – and one from Riyad Mahrez made the scoreline look more emphatic. Once you get to the fifth round of the FA Cup, it feels like you are getting within touching distance of Wembley. Because our next game was the return of the Champions League, there was also a real competition for places from those who'd been selected for the game at Newport. The Welsh team played, as all lower-division teams do, as if their lives depended on it. They didn't make it easy for us. Even as the teams shook hands before kick-off, we could see that they were a physically imposing team and the game was to be played on a surface that wasn't in the pristine condition we were used to in the Premier League.

This game was played at the stage of the season where we'd lost to Wigan during the Centurions season, so being level at 0–0 at half-time might have given encouragement to our hosts, especially as they had come closest to scoring. Any nerves from our team were lessened by a Leroy Sane goal soon after the break and from that point we settled into our stride a bit more and went on to book our place in the quarter-finals.

Champions League Round of 16 (First Leg)
Wednesday 20 February
Arena Auf Schalke
Attendance: 54,417

SCHALKE 04   **2**
Bentaleb (38, 45)

MANCHESTER CITY   **3**
Aguero (18), Sane (85), Sterling (90)

City: Ederson, Kyle Walker, Nicolas Otamendi, Aymeric Laporte, Fernandinho, Ilkay Gundogan, David Silva, Kevin de Bruyne, Raheem Sterling, Sergio Aguero, Bernardo Silva

Subs used: Vincent Kompany, Leroy Sane, Oleksandr Zinchenko

Unused subs: Arijanet Muric, Phil Foden, Riyad Mahrez, Danilo

Booked: Ederson, Fernandinho

Red Card: Otamendi

This was the return of the Champions League and, despite being in the thick of a very intense title race, four days from the Carabao Cup final and in the latter stages of the FA Cup, there was no chance to ease off here. Whenever you come up against any of the German clubs, you know you'll face an intense atmosphere, and so it was in Gelsenkirchen. I had experience of playing there for City during my first season at the club when we beat them 2–0 in the Europa League. Schalke were having a poor season in the Bundesliga so for them the pressure was off, which meant they were potentially very dangerous opponents.

In their domestic league they had been struggling to score goals, but they scored from two first-half penalties, after Sergio had given us the lead from David Silva's pass. VAR was involved in making the decision that Nico had handled, when most onlookers believed he was moving his arm behind his back when it struck him, so it seemed doubly harsh that he was also booked for this incident. After the game, Pep was asked what he thought of the decision, 'It's a penalty. I'm a big fan of VAR, it's a penalty.' There was even debate over their second penalty, given when Fernandinho pulled back Salif Sane, but some thought he might have been offside. The penalty was again converted and we went in 2–1 down and no one was really sure how that had happened.

Pep had no argument with Nico's sending off either when he was shown a second yellow card for a challenge near the halfway line, so if we were going to win this game we'd have to come from behind with just ten men on the field. We had to change things at the back, so I came on for David Silva. Still we pressed forward to see if we could find an equaliser.

It came from Leroy's brilliant free kick against his old club just a few minutes after he came on, levelling things with five minutes to go. But, such was the belief in this team, we felt there would still be time for a winner. A precision long ball from Ederson set up Raheem, who made it look very easy to finish. It meant that eventually we came back from Germany with the result we deserved, but it had been hard work.

Carabao Cup Final
Sunday 24 February
Wembley Stadium
Attendance: 81,775

CHELSEA	**0**
MANCHESTER CITY	**0**

Manchester City won 4–3 on penalties,
after extra time

City: Ederson, Kyle Walker, Nicolas Otamendi, Aymeric Laporte, Oleksandr Zinchenko, Fernandinho, Kevin de Bruyne, Bernardo Silva, David Silva, Raheem Sterling, Sergio Aguero

Subs used: Vincent Kompany, Ilkay Gundogan, Leroy Sane, Danilo

Unused subs: Arijanet Muric, Phil Foden, Riyad Mahrez

Booked: Fernandinho, Otamendi

Before this game I remember the thought going through my mind that this was the first final at Wembley that I wasn't going to start in for City. Later in the season, I didn't start the FA Cup semi-final against Brighton either, and it reminded me that age was starting to catch up with me and I was no longer guaranteed to start these big games. I understood this and I was still involved in some of them, but City had become such a big club that competition for places was very high.

When I knew that I wasn't going to start this game, it just hit me. It showed me that times were changing. Not being involved from the start was hard for me, but as captain I still had to be positive and try to remember to do a speech before the game. I wanted my teammates to do well, of course, and so all I concentrated on was being ready to play my part on the pitch if I came on. As it happened, Aymeric had a little problem at half-time and I ended up playing for almost ninety minutes because the game went to extra time. That goes to show that you can't complain for too long, because another chance always comes along and then you've just got to take it.

Clear-cut chances to score were few and far between in this game. Sergio had a goal ruled out by VAR for offside, but it was only by a bootlace. For them, N'Golo Kante had a shot over the bar. In extra time, Raheem caused panic in the Chelsea goalmouth and Kun produced a good save from Kepa. That was that, though: a very different game than when we'd beaten them 6–0 at the Etihad Stadium a couple of weeks earlier in the Premier League.

I suppose the incident that will be best remembered from the Carabao Cup final happened during the last few moments of extra time. With the scoreline still 0–0, it seemed the Chelsea goalkeeper Kepa, who'd been struggling with cramp, was about to be replaced by Willy Caballero, our former keeper. Willy was the City hero during our 2016 Capital One Cup win against Liverpool, when he'd saved three penalties, but Kepa seemed to refuse to come off. The Chelsea manager, Maurizio Sarri, was furious on the touchline and Kepa would not go even when some of his teammates tried to usher him from the field. It was completely chaotic, and I can't remember having seen anything like it.

The thing that went through my mind while all that was happening was that the worst thing that could happen, from our point of view, was Willy coming on. He's a penalty specialist, we all knew that when he was at City. We really didn't want him to come on. We thought it might have been a very smart plan by Chelsea anyway to bring him on in the last couple of minutes of extra time, ready for the penalties. They had the option of bringing on an extra substitute, so it seemed likely they'd do that, especially as Willy knew so many of us well, so had inside knowledge of our penalty-taking abilities, which might have given him an advantage.

When he didn't come on, I think we all saw that as a sign. If he'd come on our confidence would have dropped by 20 per cent; instead it got lifted by 50 per cent. When I look back at it now, it's a lesson I'm taking into management. As a manager on the touchline, I won't be allowing a player out on the pitch to overrule my decision. As a young goalkeeper I'm sure Kepa would have learned a lot from that incident, too. It was the defining moment of that game by far.

They didn't need me to take a penalty that day, but I would have been ready to take one. I'd have been very confident about scoring my first penalty, because I've been practising penalties all my career. As long as the keeper hadn't been watching videos of those, I would be confident. During my fifteen years of practising, I always hit my penalties to the same side of the keeper. I'd have been more nervous if I'd ever had to take a second penalty, but that has never happened.

Kepa had to redeem himself, and though he saved Leroy's effort, the third in our shoot-out, by then Chelsea were already behind. He'd had his chance with our second penalty, from Aguero, who had been relieved to see his kick find the net as Kepa went the right way but couldn't quite keep it out. When David Luiz hit his penalty wide it gave us the advantage again and Raheem was as cool as you like with the final penalty, which proved to be the match winner.

I remember as we celebrated with the City fans that I held up four fingers. We'd won the League Cup four times during my time at the club, which is something to be proud of. The ever-smiling Bernardo Silva bubbled after the game, 'We're very happy with the win. Another trophy for us and hopefully many more to come. It wasn't a very easy game for us. I think that physically they were stronger than us, especially in extra time. After we beat them 6–0, we knew it would be a much harder game but it's so important to win another trophy and it's a big boost for the rest of the season. I feel the love from the City fans; I think they like me a lot here. I just hope we can win many more titles together. Hopefully many, many more years to come like this.'

Pep takes all trophies very seriously and was determined,

as we all were, that this game wouldn't be dismissed. After their embarrassment in the Premier League, I can imagine how intense the Chelsea dressing room would have been before this game. They were not going to let that happen again and they didn't. It was a tough final and a slog with extra time, but we won in the end, so at this stage we had one trophy in the bag and we were still going strong in all the others.

Premier League (28)
Wednesday 27 February
Etihad Stadium
Attendance: 53,528

MANCHESTER CITY   1
Aguero (59)

WEST HAM UNITED   0

City: Ederson, Danilo, Vincent Kompany, Nicolas Otamendi, Oleksandr Zinchenko, Ilkay Gundogan, Kevin de Bruyne, David Silva, Riyad Mahrez, Sergio Aguero, Leroy Sane

Subs used: Raheem Sterling, Bernardo Silva, Phil Foden

Unused subs: Arijanet Muric, Kyle Walker, Philippe Sandler, Benjamin Mendy

Booked: None

We'd played at Wembley in a final just three days before this game, so it was always going to be tricky. It had become a recurring theme that teams would come to the Etihad and try to shut down the way we played. Usually, we eventually found a way to break through them and then the game changed. We had chances to win this game – we always did with Sergio, Raheem and David in the team – but it was won by a penalty given for a foul on Bernardo, converted by Aguero.

We were in a great rhythm – this was our fifteenth victory in sixteen games since the defeat at Leicester on Boxing Day. Despite that, you could sense the tension among City fans, who knew we couldn't afford to drop points in any game from now on. This win against West Ham proved to be the first of five 1–0 wins from our remaining eleven games, which shows how tight things were becoming.

Liverpool had drawn at an injury-hit Manchester United on the day we won the Carabao Cup at Wembley, so they'd gone above us again, but only by one point with the same number of games played. Tottenham were now five points behind us. It felt like a two-horse race for the Premier League title, especially after Liverpool beat Watford 5–0 on the same day to maintain their lead, but you couldn't completely rule out Tottenham, especially as we still had to play them at the Etihad Stadium.

As the old cliché goes, you take one game at a time, but if you looked ahead to the remaining three months of the season there were going to be a lot of vital games in April. First we had to negotiate March with three Premier League games, an FA Cup sixth-round tie and the second leg of our last-sixteen tie with Schalke in the Champions League. There could be no room for error if we wanted to win all the trophies we were playing for.

CHAPTER 8

MARCH 2019

Premier League (29)
Saturday 2 March
Vitality Stadium
Attendance: 10,699

AFC BOURNEMOUTH	0
MANCHESTER CITY	1

Mahrez (55)

City: Ederson, Kyle Walker, John Stones, Nicolas Otamendi, Oleksandr Zinchenko, Ilkay Gundogan, Kevin de Bruyne, Bernardo Silva, David Silva, Sergio Aguero, Raheem Sterling

Subs used: Riyad Mahrez, Vincent Kompany, Gabriel Jesus

Unused subs: Arijanet Muric, Danilo, Phil Foden, Leroy Sane

Booked: Walker, Otamendi

Having played the full ninety minutes against West Ham, I was back on the bench for this one. I came on as a substitute for John Stones early in the second half as we won 1–0 again. Having done what we needed to do, we watched Liverpool's derby game at Everton with interest the following day, knowing that if they didn't win, the ball was in our court again. It was so nerve-racking, especially when Liverpool created one-on-ones with Pickford. We all remembered the late mistake he'd made at Anfield when Liverpool scored their winner, but I feel like we should give him more credit for what he did at Goodison.

When the final whistle went, Everton had drawn 0–0 with Liverpool and he'd been a big part of preventing them from scoring. That result meant the outcome of the title race was back in our own hands. I was still backing us to win all our remaining games and get to ninety-eight points and now suddenly if we could achieve that points tally we would be champions again.

As far as I was concerned, that wasn't a problem. I never imagined they would get to ninety-seven. I expected they might manage ninety-one or ninety-two as the pressure mounted, and we'd still win it even if we failed to win every game. But all the other slips that I'd imagined from them never happened. That makes you realise, as if you needed reminding, how close the margins were during this season and just how good Liverpool were.

For that reason alone, this campaign felt better than any other season. It was so draining – I think by this stage we were that tired mentally that we barely had the energy to celebrate our victories. We did have a good get-together at the end of the campaign, don't get me wrong, but I remember when winning the league during the Centurions season that we actually got tired of going out and celebrating after a victory. We'd won it by the middle of April, so after that we were just waiting for the World Cup. By the time we finally reached it in the summer, that competition gave us all something serious to play for again.

This time, we would end up with only two points fewer than during that Centurions season, and yet we didn't go out to celebrate once along the way because the pressure was so intense. You couldn't even afford to go out socially with family and friends. So, although we knew that the Liverpool result left the title race in our hands, there were no thoughts of celebrating the moment – there was too much work still to be done and plenty of potential hazards along the way.

I remember feeling nervous when I saw other lads going out to restaurants, even if it was just for a meal with their family. Should they be doing that while we're in such a close title race? That's how many of us were all feeling at the time. Everyone was keeping each other in check and together so that we were ready to keep pushing. It was so relentless and tiring that when we won games we felt more relief that we had completed another part of the job than happiness for our victories.

Premier League (30)
Saturday 9 March
Etihad Stadium
Attendance: 54,104

MANCHESTER CITY   **3**
Sterling (46, 50, 59)

WATFORD   **1**
Deulofeu (66)

City: Ederson, Kyle Walker, Vincent Kompany, Nicolas Otamendi, Oleksandr Zinchenko, Ilkay Gundogan, Bernardo Silva, David Silva, Riyad Mahrez, Raheem Sterling, Sergio Aguero

Subs used: Leroy Sane, Gabriel Jesus, Phil Foden

Unused subs: Arijanet Muric, Danilo, Aymeric Laporte, Fabian Delph

Booked: Walker

For long periods of this game, Watford were set up to defend on the edge of their box and they managed to keep us out for the whole of the first half. Funnily enough, I had a few moments in this game when I thought, *I'm that close to the goal here, I should really shoot.* But my teammates were always telling me not to go for goal, so I resisted the temptation, recycled the ball and we passed it around. And, for me, that meant I linked up with one person in particular.

During Fernandinho's absences throughout the season, we saw something really quite special from Ilkay Gundogan. If people don't realise how good he is, then the way he stepped into such an important role in the team should have made it clear to everyone. What he did for the team during the last two months of the season was amazing. We won fourteen Premier League games on the bounce without the one player that, hands down, everybody in the team didn't think we could cope without: Fernandinho.

If David Silva was missing, we felt he could be replaced by Kevin de Bruyne, and, if Bernardo Silva was out, then Riyad Mahrez could step in, or Leroy Sane or Raheem Sterling. We all agreed that you wouldn't want to lose top players like Kevin, but we believed there were ways we would cope, even if it wasn't what we wanted to happen. Maybe Sergio Aguero was the other player who would have caused us problems if he'd been missing. But if you asked the fans and journalists, they all thought that Dinho was our one irreplaceable player. There didn't seem to be anyone who could fit into his shoes. He was unique. Yet Gundogan came in and proved everyone wrong.

There's no doubt that Gundo is a different type of player, with his own skill set, but actually he made the position his own during the latter part of the season. What an incredible transition that was. I think some people underestimated him, but to do what he did was not easy.

I found the whole situation funny because I had a real connection with Dinho, even more so on the pitch, because of the number of passes we made to each other during a game; it was amazing how often we would find each other. Rather than running into positions to make things happen, we would pass each other into positions all the time. There was a rhythm to it: pass, pass, pass, all short passes. We just enjoyed passing the ball to one another five, six, seven times before someone then jumped out to us and we'd then pass a triangle around the opponent.

I would feed him the ball in any position and he would just send it back to me. I was playing on the side of him and it was getting back to him and he could direct the play from there. I really enjoyed that. When he first arrived at the club, I was still recovering from my injury in Madrid so I made my reintroduction to the side at about the same time as he recovered from the injury he had at the time he joined.

We met each other for the first time in hospital. He was in one bedroom and I was in the other. One thing I noticed immediately was that he was on the phone to Pep a few times, while I was sat in the other bedroom. I never really made calls like that, so I was laughing to myself about the situation. He didn't know me at the time and he must have been thinking, *This is the former captain, he's probably the guy who's not going to be part of the plans for next season.* I was sure he must have been thinking like that.

We spoke a lot during that period, but I always had it in my mind that he thought I wouldn't be around much the following season because of my injuries. There was also the fact that Pep was a new manager with new ideas. All this was happening while Harty was being removed and there was discussion about Aguero's future, so it was natural to think that I was the next one on the list to go, especially as I was injured. I was starting, as it so often seemed, from a massive underdog position. But before he leapt to any assumptions, I said to him in hospital, 'You don't know me yet, but you will be surprised, I promise you.'

We've now got a really good friendship, but in our first sessions as we came back from injury, I just smashed him. I was so eager to prove that everything that was going to happen in the future was going to be on my terms. I was smashing into everyone in training once I was back among the squad. It was probably the worst time to do that, but

I was like an animal. After I clattered into him, especially because we'd had that conversation in hospital, I saw him giving me a look. As we recovered from our injuries together, that special relationship grew from then on. I just looked him back in the eye, laughing, and said, 'I told you you'd be surprised.'

I know deep down in his mind he never saw me as a ball-playing defender, although I was exactly that. When I was a kid, I was one of the most highly rated ball-playing defenders in Europe. I'd had to adapt my game because of injuries and then Mancini came in and imposed a completely different style to my game when he managed the club up to 2013. Therefore, Gundo wouldn't have seen what I could do.

We then went on to have this great partnership where we passed to each other so much, which I found quite funny. Despite all those preconceived ideas, he must have finally realised I was actually a good passer of the ball. He's never admitted it, but I know that's what he'd thought. I don't mind – I believe that you are always better off starting from a position where you are underestimated, rather than where too much is expected.

The win against Watford provided a lot of discussion about our first goal. Raheem was in an offside position when Sergio flicked it on towards him, but the ball deflected off Daryl Janmaat, hit Raheem and went into the goal. The assistant flagged for offside, but the referee had a long discussion with him before allowing it. If there was some controversy over that one, there was no doubt about the next two he scored to complete a fantastic thirteen-minute hat-trick, taking us four points clear at the top of the

Premier League table – if only until Liverpool played again twenty-four hours later. Playing first again gave us that slight psychological advantage.

Champions League Round of 16 (Second Leg)
Tuesday 12 March
Etihad Stadium
Attendance: 51,518

MANCHESTER CITY	**7**

Aguero (35, 38), Sane (42), Sterling (56),
Bernardo Silva (71), Foden (78), Jesus (84)

SCHALKE 04	**0**

City: Ederson, Kyle Walker, Aymeric Laporte, Oleksandr Zinchenko, Danilo, Ilkay Gundogan, Bernardo Silva, David Silva, Raheem Sterling, Leroy Sane, Sergio Aguero

Subs used: Phil Foden, Gabriel Jesus, Fabian Delph

Unused subs: Arijanet Muric, John Stones, Danilo, Eric Garcia

Booked: Danilo, Zinchenko

Schalke were a club in turmoil by the time we played them in this second leg. Their young coach, Domenico Tedesco, was under enormous pressure because of the club's lowly position in the Bundesliga. Ordinarily, a game at this stage of the Champions League against a big German club like Schalke would be won by one goal, one piece of brilliance, so tight were the margins of victory. These were not typical circumstances and Schalke looked like a team that were beaten before they even took to the field at the Etihad Stadium.

It's true that it took more than half an hour before we scored, and that was a penalty from Kun, but once we got our first they seemed to give up and the goals started to flow. Leroy Sane once again enjoyed the game against his former club, scoring a beauty himself before setting up Raheem for a tap-in with an inch-perfect cross, plus also assisting Bernardo and Phil Foden as we headed towards City's record victory in the Champions League.

Pep the perfectionist still found something to improve after the game when he told the press, 'We didn't start well, we were a bit scared to play, but after we took the lead we relaxed and decided to play and be aggressive. Everyone has to compete with each other to play. Everybody tried to play and to be bold and keep going.'

We got another glimpse of the future in this game, because VAR was used by the match officials to scrutinise several incidents. Ultimately those delays had no impact on the outcome of the game and we won the match comfortably, but they certainly frustrated the crowd, who were irritated by the long delays between some of the goals being scored and then being confirmed as being legal. We were flying again, scoring goals and advancing on all fronts.

FA Cup Sixth Round
Saturday 16 March
Liberty Stadium
Attendance: 19,783

SWANSEA CITY	**2**

Grimes (20), Celina (29)

MANCHESTER CITY	**3**

Bernardo Silva (69), Nordfeldt o.g. (78),
Aguero (88)

City: Ederson, Kyle Walker, Nicolas Otamendi, Aymeric Laporte, Fabian Delph, Ilkay Gundogan, Bernardo Silva, David Silva, Riyad Mahrez, Gabriel Jesus, Leroy Sane

Subs used: Oleksandr Zinchenko, Raheem Sterling, Sergio Aguero

Unused subs: Arijanet Muric, Danilo, Eric Garcia, Phil Foden

Booked: Laporte

While VAR was being used during the latter stages of the Champions League, for our FA Cup tie at Swansea it was not, even though other games being played at the same stage of the competition had it. It seems that VAR can only be used at stadiums fitted with the appropriate technology. This turned out to have quite a bearing on the outcome. We fell behind to Swansea and were 2–0 down at the break, but the introduction of Sergio, Raheem and Oleks turned momentum back in our favour in the second half.

The goal that drew us level came after Raheem Sterling

was brought down in the penalty area and Kun scored off the post from the spot. The argument was that the Swansea defender had got the ball before bringing down Raheem, and had VAR been available in the stadium the penalty would not have been given. To add to the controversy, the goal that won it showed Sergio in what appeared to be an offside position as he headed home Bernardo's cross in the last couple of minutes. VAR would probably have ruled that goal out, too. As a player, you try not to let these things play on your mind. I couldn't do anything about whether or not VAR was in operation, or whether we benefited from marginal decisions; all we could do was to try to win the game and play by the rules and circumstances as they were that day.

Generally, I'm a fan of progress, as I don't think you can live in the past. VAR is a step in the right direction, but it also seems incredibly clear to me that at the moment there's still a lot of work to be done with how it is used. It had to happen, but with these kinds of big changes you will always experience teething problems once it's fully introduced, which of course it wasn't here. It's early days yet.

There's no doubt that Swansea took us by surprise, but ultimately if you look at the number of chances we created in that game, luck was on the side of the team that created twenty or thirty clear chances. It certainly wasn't the other way around. Swansea played unbelievably well at times, also the way that they pressed us. They were really at the races that day; however, once we had got past them our treble dream was still alive as we were now just one game away from a second cup final of the season.

Premier League (31)
Saturday 30 March
Craven Cottage
Attendance: 25,001

FULHAM   **0**

MANCHESTER CITY   **2**
Bernardo Silva (5), Aguero (27)

City: Ederson, Kyle Walker, Nicolas Otamendi, Aymeric Laporte, Oleksandr Zinchenko, Ilkay Gundogan, Kevin de Bruyne, Bernardo Silva, David Silva, Raheem Sterling, Sergio Aguero

Subs used: Gabriel Jesus, Fernandinho, Riyad Mahrez

Unused subs: Arijanet Muric, Danilo, John Stones, Leroy Sane

Booked: None

This game came just after the passing of Bernard Halford, who'd been the club secretary at City since the 1972–73 season. Bernard was known by many fans as 'Mr Manchester City' and had worked tirelessly behind the scenes, witnessing the arrival and departure of every City manager and player since the early 1970s. He worked on and saw all the huge changes that happened at the club. I wasn't at Craven Cottage, but I'm certain it meant a lot for those that were. Bernie was my link to the history of the club. From time to time, I'm asked to talk to groups about City and what the club means to me and it's because of people like

Bernie that I can do that. He passed on so much knowledge to me.

Since I came to the club in 2008, I have made it my mission to connect with City, not just as a player but in a much deeper way. There are times when I talk to people about the club and I wanted to have a fuller understanding than simply my decade at City. It's because of Bernard, Carla, my wife, and people like Les Chapman that I feel connected with the Manchester City of twenty or thirty years ago. I really do feel like I share that history and what it was like going through those moments.

I was always amazed by the number of roles Bernie had at the club during his long time there. He was everything. These days, we have department after department to run all the different aspects of the club, but during most of his time he ran everything. He kept handwritten records in books, just like in the old days. There was no software to do things for him, nothing. He was such an important person at City. Despite what some people might think, City were already doing big things in those days. I was astonished by how far football has come since he started at the club in the early 1970s and how he managed to stay in the game so long.

If I can be a little philosophical about life here, I'd say we become who we are as people through absorbing the memories and experiences we pass down to one another, from generation to generation. Bernard entrusted me with his memories, and now I'm able to tell those same stories to people who would never have come into contact with him or what he experienced. That's what a club is about, that's what life is about. It's how a club culture develops. It really is as simple as that. I've picked things up from Bernard, who lived and breathed the club for over forty years, and I've passed all that knowledge, that life experience, that City knowledge to players as they grew into the City family, such as an 18-year-old who's just starting playing for the Blues.

I remember when we did my first FA Cup lift at City, back in 2011. That linked to Bernie as well. The club invited him to become the first non-player or manager to lift the trophy at Wembley. He'd remembered watching Stanley Matthews do that in 1953, and fifty-eight years later he did it himself. By that time, he'd already become the only non-player elected to the City's Hall of Fame, in 2006.

He wore the red and black scarf as he lifted the FA Cup and he'd always explain to everyone why he chose to wear red and black. I can remember players asking me about it at the time saying, 'Hold on a second, why is he wearing red and black? Isn't that a United colour?' Bernie told everyone that it was the kit we were wearing when we won the FA Cup in 1969 and all the different stories attached to that kit. Once he'd explained things, it made sense to everyone. I love celebrating the history of City and hope other players will carry on maintaining that sort of tradition. That's how Bernie lives on. We all move forward into the next generation because of these things.

On such a significant day, it was appropriate – maybe it was fate – that Bernardo scored our opening goal after just five minutes to set us on our way. Bernie would have found that coincidence funny. The win took us back to the top of the Premier League table, though by now we knew that if we won all our remaining games we would be champions again so that's all we concentrated on. We didn't really need to worry about Liverpool's results.

This game was played after the final international break of the season, so from now on it would be full intensity all the way as we continued to strive for all the trophies. The month of April was going to be decisive, with Tottenham coming up in the Champions League quarter-finals, an FA Cup semi-final against Brighton at Wembley, and five Premier League games, including a Manchester derby. As a footballer, it's challenges like that, and months like that, that you live for.

CHAPTER 9

APRIL 2019

Premier League (32)
Wednesday 3 April
Etihad Stadium
Attendance: 53,559

MANCHESTER CITY	2

De Bruyne (6), Sane (44)

CARDIFF CITY	0

City: Ederson, Danilo, John Stones, Aymeric Laporte, Oleksandr Zinchenko, Fernandinho, Kevin de Bruyne, Phil Foden, Riyad Mahrez, Gabriel Jesus, Leroy Sane

Subs used: Kyle Walker

Unused subs: Arijanet Muric, Vincent Kompany, Ilkay Gundogan, Bernardo Silva, David Silva, Raheem Sterling

Booked: None

This was an eighth successive win for us in the Premier League. Cardiff were fighting a relegation battle and didn't really offer much resistance, so this was a fairly straightforward win. It was inevitable that Pep would make full use of the squad with the FA Cup semi-final at Wembley coming up the following weekend.

Phil Foden got his first start in the Premier League, although it was Kevin de Bruyne who captured the headlines with an early goal from Aymeric Laporte's pass and a top-quality performance. Leroy Sane doubled the lead just before half-time, with an emphatic finish after he was set up by Gabriel Jesus. I was on the bench for this win which saw us go back to the top.

Pep praised the strength of his squad and singled out Phil in particular, 'He played excellent. He won a lot of balls in the right position. He's ready and we know it and he can play in any games in any position.' He'd twice been denied by superb saves from their keeper and we could have had more goals; at the other end, we were barely threatened.

Some City fans have told me that as each match went by they felt the title race was increasingly reported in the media from a Liverpool perspective. I never took much interest in how the media told the story. The one thing I noticed during the 2014 title race with Liverpool was that they seemed to get the support of the public more than us.

During this last season I didn't sense that they had the same level of support as 2014. That season under Brendan Rodgers, when we had Manuel Pellegrini as manager, I felt everyone wanted Liverpool to win. I heard the expression 'the people's champions' a lot. Last season was very different. I felt we had a lot of support from the red side of Manchester. It might sound weird to say this, but it seemed that they wanted us to go and win the title. I do think that incident where our bus was smashed in the Champions League changed the way that a lot of neutrals looked at Liverpool.

I don't know if my perception of things is accurate, but that's how I felt. It certainly changed the way we saw games against them from that moment on. It became even more important to us to win our games against Liverpool. My father-in-law is a United fan and he certainly wanted us to win the title again. When we lost to Liverpool in the Champions League, he appeared more disappointed than me. Don't get me wrong, I was feeling down, but he was supporting City just to stop Liverpool from going through.

Rivalry between fans should always be friendly and under those circumstances there's nothing wrong with some amicable banter between fans of different teams. During this hard-fought title race, we helped United fans stop Liverpool. It kept them on top of their rivalry with each other. We got caught in the middle of it. It's funny, because I remember during 2012 when we first won the league that I was getting a lot of messages from Liverpool fans telling me that we had to beat United to the title. They didn't want Fergie to win another one as they didn't want them to reach twenty league titles.

Indeed, during that 2012 season, it felt that neutrals from all over England were saying they didn't want United to win another league title. As the years have gone by, we've ended up in this surreal position where we had the whole of Manchester, reds included, wanting us to do well when Liverpool were our main rivals. We knew it wasn't because they really were supporting us, but because they just didn't want their big rivals to win it.

As we got closer to the end of the season, I couldn't walk around in Manchester without getting blues and reds coming up to me and saying, 'Don't let Liverpool win it.' It's just how it is living in Manchester. It's that Manc and Scousers thing, which is sometimes a bit tongue-in-cheek, but to me it just adds to the beauty of football. Those rivalries exist because our cities are so close to each other. In Manchester it's 'make sure the Scousers don't win it', and over there I'm sure it's the other way around. The twist is that I got contacted by loads of Evertonians as well during this title race. I remember that well.

I found it quite funny to witness, but overall we were just focused on what we had to do and we knew we were doing it for ourselves and the City supporters. Eventually there'll come a time when other supporters won't want us to win. That's what happens when you keep winning trophies.

I didn't play in this game against Cardiff, but I was well aware of the upcoming FA Cup semi-final against Brighton. However, I could sense that the players had successfully put that game to the back of their minds for now. Getting the win, getting the three points was all that mattered at this moment. We were one step closer to our goal – now it was time to get ready for the Cup.

FA Cup Semi-Final
Saturday 6 April
Wembley Stadium
Attendance: 71,521

BRIGHTON & HOVE ALBION   0

MANCHESTER CITY   1
Jesus (4)

City: Ederson, Kyle Walker, Nicolas Otamendi, Aymeric Laporte, Benjamin Mendy, Ilkay Gundogan, Kevin de Bruyne, Bernardo Silva, David Silva, Gabriel Jesus, Raheem Sterling

Subs used: Danilo, Fernandinho, John Stones

Unused subs: Arijanet Muric, Phil Foden, Riyad Mahrez, Leroy Sane

Booked: Walker, Danilo

The first season we played in the FA Cup semi-final, against United back in 2011, I remember being very nervous, in fact most of us were. We realised the significance of it: it gave us the chance to take the next step as a team and as a football club. I wasn't involved in this game against Brighton, but I can tell you that the attitude of the players and the whole club had totally changed. We were very calm.

Brighton made it hard for us; they're a Premier League team so we expected them to make it tough. We'd got to the stage where we knew that any game could go right down to the wire and we always prepared for that possibility. I've come to believe that even if the game involves extra time or any of the other twists and turns that happen, we could always find a way to win. In this game, we were 1–0 up after Gabriel scored in the first few minutes. Once we had a lead like that, I always felt very comfortable. We knew that even if they had levelled things at 1–1 we'd have tired them out, so another thirty minutes of play will always be in our favour.

With the team we had, and City still have, I always feel confident. It was City's fourth appearance of the season at Wembley, so we knew the environment well. I believe this was only Brighton's fourth game there in the club's history. We controlled the game once Gabriel had scored the only goal, though I do remember that Brighton, with nothing to lose, threw everything forward in the last five minutes, but we held on to book our place at Wembley for the FA Cup final.

Gabriel summed up how we all felt when he said, 'I'm so happy because we will go to another final. I want to go to the pitch and score in every game; sometimes I can't do that, but I'm happy when we win a game that was as hard as this one. Brighton were dangerous in set pieces and long balls which made it very difficult. Benjamin Mendy was back playing and he's an amazing player and an amazing guy. We go now to the quarter-finals of the Champions League and we want to win this difficult game.'

I think it would be fair to say that we didn't celebrate too much after this win because we were well aware of the huge challenges we faced during the next few weeks, so winning that semi-final was simply job done, and on to the next big game.

Champions League Quarter-Final (First Leg)
Tuesday 9 April
Tottenham Hotspur Stadium
Attendance: 60,044

TOTTENHAM HOTSPUR   1
Son (78)

MANCHESTER CITY   0

City: Ederson, Kyle Walker, Nicolas Otamendi, Aymeric Laporte, Fabian Delph, Fernandinho, Ilkay Gundogan, David Silva, Riyad Mahrez, Raheem Sterling, Sergio Aguero

Subs used: Gabriel Jesus, Leroy Sane, Kevin de Bruyne

Unused subs: Arijanet Muric, John Stones, Phil Foden, Vincent Kompany

Booked: Laporte, Mahrez

If I look back at this game as objectively as I can, I think we prepared very differently than we did for the Tottenham match at Wembley in the league. I felt like we put a lot of energy into this game before it was even played. To see that effort not get its reward was very hard for everyone.

After what happened at Anfield at the same stage of the competition the season before, we decided to be a bit more cautious. It didn't pay off. Taking the more attacking approach at Anfield the previous year hadn't worked either. That's just the way football goes sometimes. The only lessons to take out of anything that happens in life is to ask yourself: would you have done things differently? That's an answer you have to figure out for yourself. At the time of the game at Anfield, it felt like changing everything about the way we played every other week was impossible; nobody would do that.

After coming away from the Anfield Premier League game in October with a 0–0 draw by playing more cautiously, it seemed that the same approach might work at Spurs. We would have won at Anfield if the penalty had been scored, and of course we had an early penalty at Tottenham too, which Hugo Lloris saved from Aguero, so maybe everything would have been different if that had gone in. It seemed to make perfect sense to try the same thing again. We thought we could stifle out a 1–0 win and then complete the job at home, where we always play our best and just do what we do. It didn't work out that way, of course.

It was Tottenham's second game in their new stadium and their first night match there, so there was a heightened atmosphere from the start. It felt like they had an extra spring in their step. Tottenham manager Mauricio Pochettino said he thought the penalty save by his goalkeeper had given them a big lift, while Pep maintained that we'd played well and were controlling the game. He said, 'We didn't let them run a lot. If we want to progress in this competition, we have to make these kinds of comebacks [from 1–0 down]. I don't have the feeling that we played bad. We still have the second leg, it's 180 minutes. We'll see what happens, it looks a bit more complicated but every day we are going to push each other and going to try.'

It was the kind of game where chances were few and far between, so the penalty might have made a huge difference to the outcome of this game. Son Heung-Min's late goal, when he twisted into space and drove the ball in, gave them a slight advantage, but as far as we were concerned the tie was far from over. We weren't at our best that night, but we still had the second leg to turn things around. After all, a one-goal deficit was not the worst deficit to take into a home leg of a European tie.

Premier League (33)
Sunday 14 April
Selhurst Park
Attendance: 25,721

CRYSTAL PALACE   **1**
Milivojevic (81)

MANCHESTER CITY   **3**
Sterling (15, 63), Jesus (90)

City: Ederson, Kyle Walker, Vincent Kompany, Aymeric Laporte, Benjamin Mendy, Ilkay Gundogan, Kevin de Bruyne, David Silva, Raheem Sterling, Sergio Aguero, Leroy Sane

Subs used: Bernardo Silva, Gabriel Jesus, John Stones

Unused subs: Arijanet Muric, Danilo, Nicolas Otamendi, Riyad Mahrez

Booked: None

I played at the heart of the City defence alongside Aymeric for this one. It had been five years since our 2–0 win at Palace in 2014 on what had been a decisive day in the title race that season. Liverpool had been beaten by Chelsea and we went on to win the Premier League. By coincidence the same fixtures happened again, on the same day. What changed was that this time Liverpool beat Chelsea 2–0, so we had to win at Palace to maintain our one-point advantage. Having lost to them at home, we knew this was going to be a difficult match.

I gave everything I had during that game; the whole team did. Our opening goal that day was an absolute beauty with Kevin de Bruyne supplying one of those perfect through balls that he makes look so easy. Raheem raced onto it and finished in style to give us the lead on a sunny day in south London. The second goal was a sweeping team effort that saw Raheem finish a move that involved four players in the build-up, and at that point we were in control. When Palace got a goal back from a free kick with ten minutes to go, there was a little anxiety until Gabriel scored a late one to make it 3–1.

'We are happy,' said Pep. 'Five games left. The difference between this game and the match against Crystal Palace at our stadium is that in that game they shoot three times and score three goals. We knew exactly what we were playing for today. We have 183 points in two seasons in the Premier League, which is incredible. Why should we ever doubt what these players can do?'

Champions League Quarter-Final (Second Leg)
Wednesday 17 April
Etihad Stadium
Attendance: 53,348

MANCHESTER CITY	**4**

Sterling (4, 21), Bernardo Silva (11),
Aguero (59)

TOTTENHAM	**3**

Son (7, 10), Llorente (73)

City: Ederson, Kyle Walker, Vincent Kompany, Aymeric Laporte, Benjamin Mendy, Ilkay Gundogan, Kevin de Bruyne, Bernardo Silva, David Silva, Raheem Sterling, Sergio Aguero

Subs used: Fernandinho, Leroy Sane

Unused subs: Arijanet Muric, John Stones, Riyad Mahrez, Gabriel Jesus, Nicolas Otamendi

Booked: None

I'd already made my mind up that I was leaving City before this game, so I knew that we had to win this tie to keep my dream of winning the Champions League with City alive. I made the decision that my time at City was coming to an end because the force of the wheel of change I mentioned earlier was getting more and more powerful. I could try everything I had to try to slow it down, but when it's time it's time. What I didn't want to do was play on for one year too many.

By making the decision during the season, it gave me an added incentive to keep on fighting and giving everything I had, with the aim of leaving a legacy I could be proud of. I admit that a lot of the time during the campaign I was not quite the player I had been at the peak of my powers. A lot of the things that I once took for granted were not quite there any more.

I'd learned how to adapt my playing style and play to the strengths I had without over-extending myself, but I would still try to be the player that people believed I was. I don't mind risk, and in that sense I wouldn't have minded playing on for another year, but to be honest I just thought I was fighting a losing battle and if the right opportunity came along it was time to take it. My contract was due to end in the summer, and at this point I didn't have an offer on the table from City. I didn't want to run the risk of being offered a new contract out of pity. I wanted to keep everything in my own hands. It had to be my decision and not City deciding they didn't want me any more.

If I hadn't received the offer to return to Anderlecht, maybe I would have taken longer to make the decision to leave. This was the one chance I couldn't resist or refuse, as it took me back to the club where I had started and gave me the opportunity to begin the next phase of my career, as a manager. This was what I wanted. From that point onwards, I knew I was going to Anderlecht. I didn't tell anyone about my decision apart from one or two close friends in the team, but even then I don't think I said where I was going.

Although I knew this was my last chance in the

Champions League with City, I wasn't emotional playing in that game against Tottenham. I didn't let it affect me at all. My attitude was that if I wasn't going to win it with City as a player, I'd try to win it as a manager. I've got another forty years to do it now.

We knew that we would be playing Tottenham again very soon after this Champions League tie had been completed. I didn't believe that the outcome of the tie would have any bearing on the Premier League game that followed. But it turned out to be one of the most dramatic matches you could wish for.

We got off to the best possible start, as Raheem's early goal immediately cancelled out their lead from the first leg and lifted us. Kevin passed the ball out to him and he cut inside from the left and curled a shot into the goal. But the mood didn't last long as they hit back soon after through Son, who shot from the D to make it 1–1 on the night, which felt like a hammer blow. It soon got worse when we lost the ball in midfield, Moura sent the ball on to Eriksen, who set up Son. His shot was unstoppable, right into the top corner, and after ten minutes played we were 2–1 down, 3–1 on aggregate, meaning we would have to score four goals on the night to win. We didn't stop. Sergio found Bernardo Silva just outside the penalty area, and his shot was deflected off Rose and past Lloris to make it 2–2 on the night, with still only eleven minutes on the clock.

For those who say that European football can be cagey, this was anything but. As a team, as a squad, we didn't know when to give in, so when Raheem made it 3–2 from Kevin's great cross and there was still less than a quarter of the game gone, we had already felt the full range of emotions. As a player I was trying to keep mine in check, but I could imagine what the City fans in the stands must have been going through. One more goal and we'd have the overall lead.

With an hour gone we were finally ahead in the tie, after Kevin set up Kun to score to make it 4–2, but that wasn't the end of the drama by any means, though we seemed to have things more under control at last, as VAR had a decisive impact on the outcome.

As far as I'm concerned, I saw a clear handball when Fernando Llorente got the goal for Tottenham that made it 4–3 on the night. In any normal world that was a goal, but strictly by the rules, it was illegal. A Spurs corner flicked off the head of Kyle Walker, hit Llorente and then rolled over the goal line. It's a transition period for VAR, but before it came off his hip, I saw the ball hit his hand. I know he didn't do it on purpose, as I could see that his hands were by his side. At the time the rule wasn't completely clear to me, but these days the arm cannot play any part in a goalscoring situation, and maybe we should look again at the details of this rule. For me to have seen it and the referee not to spot it on the VAR remains a mystery to me to this day. How can you have so many angles and not spot that the ball went to his hand? It would have been harsh if the goal were overruled for Tottenham, but if that's the rule then that's the rule.

The year before Liverpool had been better than us in the Champions League, but who knows what would have happened if Leroy hadn't been ruled offside or if we'd got a penalty. These are the crucial moments and fine margins that can decide the outcomes of football matches at that stage of the big competitions. VAR got this one wrong, and that mistake put us out of the tie, but it wouldn't be long before it was called into use in another key moment.

Knowing we needed to score again to go through, we kept going, pressing for that vital goal. Two-and-a-half minutes into stoppage time, very reminiscent of the 'Ageroooo' goal in 2012, we got it when Raheem got the winner. Or was it? The referee called for VAR to check, and it decided that Kun was offside in the build-up. The crowd who had been roaring us on went quiet. Pep threw his lucky hoody to the floor and we were out.

It's tough as captain to be the one person that needs to stay motivated, but to lift an entire team when in the last minute of the game you've had a goal cancelled, I just knew we didn't have the time to get back up from this. It felt really strange because I saw the devastation of the Tottenham play-ers when they thought they had conceded; it looked similar to what I've seen City fans go through in previous years. They all fell on the floor, almost in tears. When Raheem scored that goal, I didn't react straightaway, although in my head I did think, *We've done it again.* I didn't overly celebrate. I stayed calm, because I feared that VAR would overturn it. Until the moment it was ruled out, I still believed we'd find a way to get the goal we needed. I knew something bad was going to happen. I was prepared for it, but at the same time was just devastated when the reality sunk in. It was the first time I thought we wouldn't go through and the whole team felt the same. My dream of winning the Champions League as a player with City was over.

It had been such an emotional game to play in. Afterwards, Ilkay Gundogan was captured on camera kneeling on the floor holding his head in his hands and you could see, from the expression on Pep's face as he left the field, that he felt upset by what happened too. It was one of those games that was like riding a rollercoaster. One minute you were up and believed that everything was possible, the next you were as low as you could go. But I knew we couldn't let the devastation affect us, we still had two more trophies to win. Focus, focus, focus.

Premier League (34)
Saturday 20 April
Etihad Stadium
Attendance: 54,489

MANCHESTER CITY   1
Foden (5)

TOTTENHAM HOTSPUR   0

City: Ederson, Kyle Walker, John Stones, Aymeric Laporte, Oleksandr Zinchenko, Ilkay Gundogan, Kevin de Bruyne, Phil Foden, Bernardo Silva, Raheem Sterling, Sergio Aguero

Subs used: Fernandinho, Leroy Sane, David Silva

Unused subs: Arijanet Muric, Nicolas Otamendi, Gabriel Jesus, Riyad Mahrez

Booked: Sterling

In some ways this was the ideal game to play next, because we knew Tottenham would be exhausted, but we also knew we could beat them because we'd won the game in the Champions League and only gone out on the away-goals rule. It might surprise you, but the fact that we'd lost the Champions League tie to Tottenham actually made me more confident about winning this Premier League game. We knew we had to be even more on it this time round. Our squad was very big and therefore able to absorb a lot of games, so we could make a few changes to the line-up (I was one of them). I thought Tottenham suffered a lot more than we did in that second leg. They'd had to hang on like you wouldn't believe. Physically, I felt the two Champions League games had been much more draining for them, which would obviously give us a big advantage in this match. We were at home again, so that would help too.

Pep had said so many times during the season that how a team reacts after a disappointment is key to how successful they can be. If you win game after game everyone is happy, but after a defeat, even if it is on the away-goals rule, it is the players who shrug it off and are ready to take risks and play with creativity and freedom again immediately who are the winners.

There were three changes to the starting line-up with Phil Foden, Oleksandr Zinchenko and John Stones coming in. Having lost the chance to win the quadruple by going out of the Champions League, it felt like today was the start of the business end of the Premier League title race. By now there was no doubt in our minds that we would have to win all five of the games we still had to play; there could be no slip-ups, not even a draw.

It didn't take long for us to get in front in this game with Bernardo crossing to Sergio, who headed across goal and there was Phil Foden to turn it in. We might have had a second from the penalty spot if the referee had seen the contact made by Jan Vertonghen on Bernardo, but it wasn't given.

Phil spoke for us all after the game when he said, 'It was a great game to play in. It was hot today. I think the early goal made it easier and once you've got that you can relax a bit more. We could sense the tension coming from the supporters in the stands, it's bound to be like that. There's a lot on the line in the Premier League. I thought the fans were great helping us but I can understand their anxiety when the score was only 1–0 for so long. We've won ten in a row, we've now got four games left and they're all going to be finals and we need to win them all. I love playing with Bernardo. I think he's the best player I've played with. He keeps the ball in tight areas and he's just a joy to play with.'

Pep said that our performance in this game was not our best, compared to the other two against Spurs: 'They had nothing to lose while we knew that we had to win if we're to retain the Premier League. The last two days, since we went out of the Champions League, have been tough, but we are still here. We have known for a while that if we lose one more game we won't win the Premier League. This Liverpool team is one of the best I have ever seen, defensively, offensively, so for us to still be there with one of the best players [Kevin de Bruyne] not there is quite remarkable. After what happened last Wednesday against a Tottenham side that is going to finish in the top four, for my players to win again is massive.'

There were five games to go, including the FA Cup final. These games were going to be special and we had much to aim for. I couldn't wait to play the next game.

Premier League (35)
Wednesday 24 April
Old Trafford
Attendance: 74,431

MANCHESTER UNITED	**0**
MANCHESTER CITY	**2**

Bernardo Silva (54), Sane (66)

City: Ederson, Kyle Walker, Vincent Kompany, Aymeric Laporte, Oleksandr Zinchenko, Fernandinho, Ilkay Gundogan, Bernardo Silva, David Silva, Raheem Sterling, Sergio Aguero

Subs used: Leroy Sane, Gabriel Jesus, Danilo

Unused subs: Arijanet Muric, Nicolas Otamendi, Phil Foden, Riyad Mahrez

Booked: Kompany, Zinchenko

I love the derby because of the banter and the rivalry. I understand that some fans might feel genuine hate for one another, but that's not what I feel. I just wanted to win that game more than any other, because I know a lot of people that are associated with United too. It goes both ways.

United fans in my family don't want me to win on derby day, even though they like me as a person. I want to win that game as much as they want their team to win it. If you live outside of Manchester, you can take things out of context sometimes and assume the relationship between all City and United fans is full of hate, but I don't think it is. I've been in Manchester a long time and I've been around normal supporters. We all love our clubs and we're all the same, talk the same, behave virtually the same, but some talk a little bit more nonsense than others. Those who do that usually wear a red shirt!

Although this was the Manchester derby, which has a significance of its own, we knew we had to win every game that we had left in the Premier League and there would be three more to play after this one. Earlier in my time at City, playing United at Old Trafford was always a huge challenge for us, but I certainly didn't see this as even the most difficult game we had left. Don't get me wrong, I have an enormous amount of respect for the United players. The individuals they have are tremendous players, and you have to acknowledge the history of their club, but at that stage, as a team, we were much further along than them. I knew we were going to do well that night at Old Trafford.

Being confident didn't guarantee we'd get the result we needed, but I had every reason to believe in the team's ability to go there and get the three points. The first half was just a case of controlling the game without taking too many risks, but once we came out for the second half we hit our stride. After the break, Bernardo, making his 100th appearance for City, scored a great individual goal in front of our travelling supporters. There was a release of emotion from the fans and we all enjoyed the skill that he'd shown to execute that goal. Leroy Sane drove in a second to ease any nerves that there might have been and we were on course to keep the winning run going.

After the game, Leroy told CityTV that he was really happy to have won the derby and such an important game in our bid to retain the Premier League. 'We need to stay focused and hungry. Now we just need to rest and get ready for Burnley because the last three games will definitely not be easy.'

It was funny that night because everybody made so much out of the fact that the United players had so much pace and I thought to myself, *This is the same mistake everybody has made about me throughout my career.* They look at pace and they look at my age and they think straightaway, *He's going to get done here.* What they forget is that there are so many other ways to deal with pace. It's not just about being as fast as the other guy, it is also about how to out-think them tactically. Get it right and you can actually give yourself a very easy game against pure speed.

Pace kept getting mentioned when people spoke about me during the end of my time at City. I'd always been fast earlier in my career, which made it easier to deal with it when I came up against speedy forwards. During that period, while I was still as quick as most, I was also learning how to counter the threat in other ways so, as I grew older and lost a bit of my own pace, I was still never done by speed. That was another reason I decided to leave City on a high, because I knew that sooner or later, even with all my experience of how to handle pace, eventually I would come up against someone who would be too fast for me. But it didn't happen in that game or at any time during my ten years at City.

I learned how to deal with quick players during the many games when I was playing at maybe 60 or 70 per cent of my full capability. I played so many games at that level that I've lost count. I got so used to playing in a way where I just needed to use my brain that people completely underestimated how comfortable and easy I found dealing with these situations.

After the game, Pep said that he felt that both City and Liverpool deserved to win the title. His attitude helped us in this situation. At half-time he'd told us, 'We have to take a chance and play to win. It doesn't matter if we lose, we have to try to win.'

Our focus now switched to the game at Burnley so he warned us, 'People will talk too much. Tomorrow we won't switch on the TV. We just have to go there and win.'

Premier League (36)
Sunday 28 April
Turf Moor
Attendance: 21,605

BURNLEY	**0**
MANCHESTER CITY	**1**
Aguero (63)	

City: Ederson, Kyle Walker, John Stones, Aymeric Laporte, Oleksandr Zinchenko, Ilkay Gundogan, Bernardo Silva, David Silva, Raheem Sterling, Sergio Aguero, Leroy Sane

Subs used: Gabriel Jesus, John Stones

Unused subs: Arijanet Muric, Danilo, Nicolas Otamendi, Phil Foden, Riyad Mahrez

Booked: Gundogan

When we looked ahead to the games left in our Premier League fixtures, as we got nearer and nearer to the end, there was still the trip to Burnley. I also told everyone who would listen to me that Leicester at home would be extremely difficult to win, but this game at Turf Moor felt like a key moment for us. The grass was quite long and dry, which slows things down and meant our passing couldn't be quite as slick as usual. We felt they used every tactic they knew to try to get cheap fouls. They were diving and complaining to the referee and trying to turn the game into a dog fight. A game featuring lots of set pieces, stop-start, suited their game plan.

They were legitimate tactics designed to make the game difficult for us. Let's be honest, every team has their own way of playing and they were entitled to try whatever they thought would help them win, or at least not lose, in front of their own supporters. It was a tactic that had worked for them before and they could be very successful at it.

Those were the antics they tried that day. It's part of football. If you miss clear chances in a game like that, which we did, and they clear shots off the line, the fear is you'll get done on a throw-in or something like that. Players can get turned, in comes a cross and suddenly you're in trouble. I felt it was a major achievement to go there that day and get the result that we needed.

I've still never seen the goal that Sergio Aguero scored to get the win at Burnley, apart from on the day itself. I've said many times that Pep is able to make every player better, but with Sergio it's harder to say, because his level was already so high when Pep arrived. With every other player, I can pinpoint so many things that he helped players improve, but in the case of Kun things were simpler: in my eyes he just had to maintain his level.

The one thing that has improved in his game is the way he holds onto the ball. I think Sergio did this himself, so he should take the credit. I remember at the beginning of his City career he was not as good at holding the ball up. Now he's unbelievable. He's like a magnet, the ball never leaves his foot, even when there are three or four guys around him that ball is safe at his feet. I don't know how he does it.

At the beginning of my time at City I associated that skill with Carlos Tevez. He was also unbelievable at keeping possession, which always gave the rest of the team so much room to breathe. Aguero, at that time, was not at that level. I'm not talking about his goalscoring, his speed, his actions, his dribbles, just about his hold-up play.

More recently, I remember that game against Liverpool when the ball nearly touched the sky, well, the roof of the stadium. He brought it down in front of Van Dijk in an instant, dead. He just killed it. He did that under the highest pressure, against one of the best defenders in the world. Apart from the magnificent Messi, I don't know any other player who would have been able to control the ball in those conditions at that point in the game like that.

He's a joker off the pitch, but out there he's such an intelligent player. I think those types of players just reboot and reboot again. Every single season they seem to self-improve, and he's certainly been able to do that. I've not seen him spend an incredible amount of time with coaches, I've just seen him improve – God knows how he does it.

Sergio is seen as the number one by so many people and it's hard to argue against that. I definitely think he deserves that accolade, even though David Silva is unbelievable and Yaya Toure has given us some amazing moments. However, I think we need to wait a few years and then reflect as to who is really the best. Aguero is still active and he's doing so much right now, but I think in a few years' time we'll have a better idea of how it'll all be finally assessed.

We couldn't have achieved the titles we have without Yaya, we couldn't have done it without Sergio or without David, even without Joe. When it comes down to it, though, Kun stands out because scoring is the hardest part of football and he's done it so prolifically, so he might just edge it because of that. The truth is that so many players have made such a great impact.

David is generally more introverted than Sergio. He doesn't do interviews in English, so maybe you don't hear from him as much, but if you can speak or read Spanish, I think he makes himself quite accessible and has lots of opinions. His English is actually very good, so I don't know why he doesn't talk more in that language, but they are two very different people. Sergio enjoys everything. He can have fun at a commercial photo shoot – that kind of thing – whereas David will try to get out of things like that as soon as he can.

So here we were, on the verge of achieving a domestic treble, which no club had ever done before. It was all to come in May, and these would be my last games as a Manchester City player. It was all in our own hands. We 'just' had to win three more games. Would I play in them all, could I help to make the difference, could I score a key goal and would I get the chance to end my time at City in the perfect way by lifting the two major trophies that lay ahead of us? What a month May 2019 promised to be, but nothing could be taken for granted; we would have to be at our very best. Big challenges awaited us.

CHAPTER 10

MAY 2019

Premier League (37)
Monday 6 May
Etihad Stadium
Attendance: 54,506

MANCHESTER CITY	1
Kompany (70)	
LEICESTER CITY	0

City: Ederson, Kyle Walker, Vincent Kompany, Aymeric Laporte, Oleksandr Zinchenko, Ilkay Gundogan, Phil Foden, Bernardo Silva, David Silva, Raheem Sterling, Sergio Aguero

Subs used: Leroy Sane, Gabriel Jesus, John Stones

Unused subs: Arijanet Muric, Danilo, Nicolas Otamendi, Riyad Mahrez

Booked: Jesus, Kompany, David Silva

I remember having a discussion with Ilkay Gundogan about how tough the Leicester game would be. We'd agreed that the Burnley game was going to be a tricky one, and the matches against Tottenham and United of course, but I stated that Leicester would be the toughest of them all, though he didn't agree. I said, 'I'm telling you, it's not the Leicester from before; this is now a Brendan Rodgers team.' I'd seen how they'd improved. I felt that, in many ways, they were doing some of the things we were doing. I was quite insistent that they were much better than the team we'd played before Rodgers took charge. Pep agreed with me and ahead of the game he gave us a warning. He basically told the team in the pre-match meeting exactly what I'd said to Ilkay. He told everyone to be careful and that we needed to be at our very best.

Once we started everyone soon agreed that it was probably the hardest we'd had to work to recover the ball in any single game all season. The Liverpool match was at a level above everything else, but the next one after that was this game against Leicester. They were tougher to play against than Arsenal, Chelsea or Tottenham.

Having the ball is a big part of our game. If we don't have the ball we are nothing like the same team. For us to eventually win that game made it even more special because I don't think everyone realised just how well they'd played. With it being on a Monday night, it felt even more dangerous than if it had been played during the afternoon the previous weekend. Those night matches when you have to win the game are not always the ones you look forward to the most.

As we stepped out onto the pitch, we knew that Liverpool

had won their game and only had one more to go, against Wolves at Anfield, the following Sunday. I knew they would win their last game so, as we'd known for many weeks, we had to beat Leicester and then finish our season with a win at Brighton on the last day of the Premier League season.

I suppose you could compare the game against Leicester with the penultimate game of the 2012 season when we played Newcastle at St James' Park and Yaya Toure scored twice in the last twenty minutes to help us to a 2–0 win. That set up the last-day drama against Queens Park Rangers and Aguero scoring the stoppage-time goal that wrote us all into the history books. Newcastle were strong that day, but we played a lot better than them, even though the goals came fairly late on. The Leicester game was much tougher for us because of the quality that they have all over the pitch.

They had Jamie Vardy leading their attack; then there was Kasper Schmeichel, who's a great goalkeeper and also has the ability to play as a sweeper keeper, plus just like Ederson or Bravo for us, he can play as a 'quarterback' and set attacks underway from the back. They had a great back four with Pereira, Evans, Maguire and Chilwell and my fellow Belgian Youri Tielemans was a key player, too. I could go right through the team because there are so many good players there, like James Maddison and of course my old teammate Kelechi Iheanacho, who, late on in the game, almost scored an equaliser after my goal had given us the lead.

I have a good sense for when key games and key moments happen. I really thought that the Leicester match was going to be gridlock, but I always believed we'd find a way to score the goal we needed because I trusted the players. We had such a great team, I knew someone would do something that would find a way through.

I must admit, though, as the game went along I'd started to think that this might be the one where it didn't happen. I knew that every corner, every set piece was a big chance that we had to be fully focused for. I knew that we had to try extra hard in these moments, especially as time ticked on.

Aguero had an effort that hit the woodwork and Gundo had a shot that went just wide. We started this game on fire. We were zinging balls around at 200mph. That wasn't enough, though, and good teams like the ones Brendan Rodgers manage slightly adapt certain players' positions so they are able to stifle us. In possession they were safe and made us do the running, more than we wanted to, which was not typical of any other team that we played against.

The game was not going in the right direction for so many reasons. It might have proved easier to put this tie to bed if we'd got an early goal. I think if we'd scored early on they would have made more mistakes and been a little less patient. I'm sure we would have capitalised on that and killed off the threat. Drawing 0–0 was perfect for them. I could sense the pressure building as we moved into the last quarter, knowing that if we didn't win Liverpool would be one victory from the title.

The strange thing was, when I woke up on the morning of the game I had a feeling that I'd do something significant or special. To be honest, though, I'd felt that way before lots of other games and it never happened, but I definitely woke up that morning thinking, *Today I'm going to do something special*. Thankfully, this time it happened.

My experience of previous seasons told me that whenever it got to these crunch games, I was usually in or around something significant. I don't know how or why that would happen. Even if you look at the Centurions season, we were supposed to win the league at the game against United, which didn't happen because we had a major collapse in the second half, but in that game I scored a goal as well. I headed it home like my life depended on it to give us the lead, despite Chris Smalling hanging onto my shirt as I battled to get to the ball. In those circumstances I always felt that nothing could stop me. In these key matches in every season I feel like I'm ready, just behind the main guy, I can jump to the front of the queue and make the difference.

With twenty minutes to go, that time came. I received a square ball from Aymeric Laporte. He simply knocked it into the space in front of me and no one immediately challenged me. I felt like I was being invited to shoot, but as it crossed my mind to hit it, I heard a shout from the player nearest to me, Ilkay Gundogan. He yelled, 'Don't shoot!' It annoyed me, so I took the shot because I was angry. I don't like being told those things – I hate it. A teammate can ask for the ball, no problem, but don't say to me, 'Don't shoot!' I never liked being told what I couldn't do from when I was very young. It was something I hated. 'Don't tell me what I can't do!' I just thought *enough is enough*, and so I went for it.

I couldn't have connected better. I couldn't have hit it more sweetly or more powerfully and I knew it was going in from the moment it left my foot. What a feeling it was when it hit the back of the net. It felt like all the tension in the stadium, in the team and in my body was released in that moment.

As a manager, I encourage everyone to shoot, all the time. The moment you stop shooting is the moment you stop scoring goals. Across the whole season you are more likely to waste the chance to score goals because of that attitude than gain anything from always being scared to have a go. That's why I always tell everyone to shoot.

It wasn't the first time I'd had an opportunity like this. I'd been in that same position against Watford earlier in the season, perhaps even closer to goal. I was getting into those positions so often that when I did I told Gundo to drop back for a minute or two to centre back, so that the other defender was not alone. In that Leicester game, Gundo had put about four shots into the second tier of the stands and so I thought, *Okay, it's not going in from him.* Yet when I had the ball in the same position he was shouting, 'Don't shoot!' I thought that was a bit rich.

The backstory to all this is that we had been doing various shooting drills in training and everyone saw it as a fluke when I won. Yet I always ended up in and around the final of those training-ground competitions, because I understood the strategy you needed to take in order to do well: you had to be in front of the right person or behind the right person. If you're behind someone who scores all the time, you have to score right after him to stay in the game or you'll be eliminated. It's hard to explain how the training situation works, but I always found a way to make sure I did well.

I always played the game a bit tactically. I'd like to think I was being clever. I'd work out who didn't have his shooting boots on that day and go behind him. That way I managed to survive, not necessarily because of pure skill, but I got through to the last few and the finals of the shooting drills.

Everybody always laughed at me. 'Why's he shooting? He's never going to shoot in a game.' But every now and again I would score an absolute screamer in training. As they laughed at me, I used to say, 'You wait, you'll see.' I've called it for ten years that one day I'd score one of those goals for real and you'll be very grateful that I practised for so many years. Against Leicester all that practice finally came off, at exactly the right time.

I know that Kev de Bruyne said I couldn't shoot, but if you look back at the goals I scored during my career from long range – I know there weren't many – they were always great strikes. With all the injuries I suffered during my career, I started to think that it was a risky part of the game for me because you can pull a muscle during the action of striking the ball with maximum power. As a defender, I didn't need to take that risk. As time went on I stopped shooting in matches completely.

I became very pragmatic because I knew there were players much better than me at shooting. I'd just pass the ball to them. If you play for a club where there are not that many players with greater ability than you, in general, you take a lot more personal responsibility. When you have players alongside you like David Silva, who was so good at the last pass, why would I attempt that perfect through ball? It was much simpler just to give it to David, who I knew could play it perfectly every time. Similarly, when you have players like Kevin, who are so good at shooting, why shoot when I could give it to Kevin?

That change happened when City became a big club

and all the players around me were capable of remarkable things. Earlier in my career, it was more usual for me to take shots or to try the last pass, because I was one of the better guys in the team. I know that I scored that special header against United with two games to go in the 2012 season, but this goal against Leicester felt better. Perhaps because I already knew I was leaving City at the end of the season.

So many of my teammates had their say about my goal afterwards. Kyle Walker said: 'I felt that a goal needed to come from outside the box, or something special or someone to put their name in the history book, hopefully.' Bernardo Silva added: 'As a team we all felt that Vinny's goal gave us the win that we needed to get the three points to go top of the league again. At that moment we just wanted to hug him and kiss him and say thank you for that goal.'

Ilkay Gundogan admitted he was glad I ignored his advice in that crucial moment. 'I was only a few yards away from him and I could tell he was thinking about a shot so I shouted, "Don't shoot!" He went ahead and shot anyway and I'm glad he did; what a goal. I'm glad he ignored me.'

Pep Guardiola had this to say: 'When Vinny got the ball I was thinking, "Don't shoot – pass the ball." He took a good decision, though. I honestly didn't have too much confidence when he chose to shoot, but that's football. I have said many times that the players are artists, they have to decide what they are going to do in fractions of a second. The important thing is that he believed and so he shot. He's a big believer so that's why he did that to help us win the game. It was an incredible goal, incredible.

'He's a real defender and a huge personality and he is beloved in the dressing room and he's a leader, which he has shown many times. He's an incredible human being. He has helped me a lot. I was always sad that I couldn't use him [on the field] more, but we know that when he was available we can always count on him. This club is what it is because of guys like Vincent.

'To be consistent every three days is difficult for him, but, when we had one game a week and he had time, Vincent was an important, incredible player. Vincent Kompany, just like Joe Hart and Pablo Zabaleta, is one of the guys that has helped this club to make a step forward. He's been here ten years. It doesn't matter how many titles he has, or if we will win in the future, he is one of the greatest players for this club, ever.'

Premier League (38)
Sunday 12 May
American Express Community Stadium
Attendance: 30,662

BRIGHTON & HOVE ALBION   1
Murray (27)

MANCHESTER CITY   4
Aguero (28), Laporte (38), Mahrez (63),
Gundogan (72)

City: Ederson, Kyle Walker, Vincent Kompany, Aymeric Laporte, Oleksandr Zinchenko, Ilkay Gundogan, Bernardo Silva, David Silva, Riyad Mahrez, Raheem Sterling, Sergio Aguero

Subs used: Kevin de Bruyne, Nicolas Otamendi

Unused subs: Arijanet Muric, Danilo, John Stones, Leroy Sane, Gabriel Jesus

Booked: None

I felt very calm and really confident as we got ready for the final Premier League game of the season. My only fear was that Brighton might try to use the tactics Burnley had used a couple of matches earlier, to try to stop us playing our usual game. In the end I needn't have had that concern, because they didn't leave the grass long or try to play for set pieces. Even when they scored first, I thought to myself that it was so early in the game that we still had plenty of time and that usually brought out the best in our team.

I had a good friend who was at Liverpool for their game against Wolves that day. After we'd won and we'd celebrated, I rang him to ask how their crowd had reacted when Brighton took the lead against us. He told me it was like a party inside the ground and that some of their supporters were crying in the stands saying, 'We're going to do it.' When I heard that, I realised that it was worth us having that scare just to spoil their day that little bit.

I remember sitting on the bench so many times earlier in the season with Riyad, telling him his time would come, and sure enough it did when he scored that crucial third goal at Brighton. I knew the title was ours again when that goal went in. The number of times he'd sat next to me, drinking a cup of coffee, watching the team win 5–0 and we'd be saying to each other, 'We're never going to play at this rate.' Those that were in the team just kept smashing everyone.

I remember the look we gave each other when he scored that goal against Brighton. He also gave a great assist in that game and I reminded him that it was those moments that sum up football. Brighton were getting hurt by us every time they tried to press, so eventually they gave up doing it. As soon as they stopped trying to press us, the game was finished.

I felt like a little kid as I lifted the Premier League trophy in front of the travelling supporters. It's like a living dream. When you look at the pictures, my face is like a child's. It's a dream come true. It's the biggest achievement you can have. The Premier League is such an imposing trophy to lift. It's heavy so I always remember thinking that the first ten seconds after you lift it are amazing and then it just becomes heavy. At that point you just want to pass it on. It's a brilliant feeling, though. I remember thinking, *Shit, I've won four now, is that a lot?* Then I remember a completely irrational thought going through my head: *I just need one more, I need to win the next one again!* I'd already decided to move to Anderlecht and leave City, but it still flashed through my mind. One thing is for sure, winning is addictive.

I grabbed some of the other players when the final whistle went and we jumped up and down together singing, 'Campeones, Campeones, Olé Olé Olé'. It's hard to put into words what those moments feel like, but as a City player, as a City fan and as a Manc it meant the world to me.

Pep was naturally very happy with our achievement, 'From

the beginning of this title race we knew that Liverpool were incredible, they played less games than us because they went out of the FA Cup and Carabao Cup quite early, but we were incredibly consistent. I think that our achievement over the last two seasons with 198 points has lifted the standard of the competition higher than it has ever gone. I have to thank Liverpool because they made us better than last season.'

After the game, we flew straight back to Manchester to celebrate with the City fans who couldn't be at Brighton with us. I told the crowd, 'We're so, so proud. This team is amazing. We're able to fill this place [the Etihad] at this time of the night [10 p.m.] and, you know what: thank you so much!'

FA Cup Final
Saturday 18 May
Wembley Stadium
Attendance: 85,854

MANCHESTER CITY   **6**
David Silva (26), Jesus (38, 68), de Bruyne
(61), Sterling (81, 87)

WATFORD   **0**

City: Ederson, Kyle Walker, Vincent Kompany, Aymeric Laporte, Oleksandr Zinchenko, Ilkay Gundogan, Bernardo Silva, David Silva, Riyad Mahrez, Raheem Sterling, Gabriel Jesus

Subs used: Kevin de Bruyne, Leroy Sane, John Stones

Unused subs: Arijanet Muric, Danilo, Sergio Aguero, Nicolas Otamendi

Booked: David Silva

It was during the week leading up to the FA Cup final, in fact the day before the last training session ahead of the game, when I finally told Pep that I would be leaving City after this game. Why did I leave it so late to tell him and the majority of the players? I wanted him to be part of the decision of how and when we communicated it to the rest of the players. I didn't want him to tell them if he thought my announcement would have a negative effect ahead of the one remaining game. If we could gain 10 per cent by telling them before, then that's what I wanted. If he thought it would have a negative effect, then I would rather tell them after the game.

I woke up on the morning of the final and I thought, *This is going to be the hardest speech I have ever done in my career.* It's the last game of the season and the season has already been so successful, so what do you say to a team that has already achieved so much so they'll be extra motivated to go and play and give everything against a team like Watford? The only thing I could think of saying was: 'Today, we're not just playing for the FA Cup, we are playing to win the English treble. It's not because of the eleven players on the pitch, it's because of every member of this team and every member of this staff. All I am asking of you, the fifty people here in this dressing room, is to push to the last, to push everyone because the English treble is in all of our names. We need everyone today to push this team over the line. Come on!'

I wasn't frightened of failure ahead of this game. I've always thrived on these moments. The more complicated the situation, the more that was riding on it, the more I trusted myself. The way Watford had played against us in the games earlier that season left me feeling confident that, apart from an occasional set piece, we didn't have too much to worry about. I knew we would dominate possession in the game and whenever you do that the probabilities are always in your favour, especially when you had players like we had who could make the difference.

The first big chance of the game fell to them, which goes to show, once again, the fine margins we are dealing with. Roberto Pereyra was clear and Ederson made a tremendous save. It was 0–0 at that stage and if that had gone in it certainly would have given Watford added belief, but I would have never doubted that we could have come from behind and won the game. As much as we dominated, we did struggle a little bit in the early stages. However, I started the game with a confident mindset and emotions didn't ever get in the way for me. I'm very lucky in that respect.

We scored goals soon after through David Silva and Gabriel Jesus, so by half-time we were well on the way to winning the FA Cup. The Watford fans were fantastic throughout. When they started singing and waving their scarves late in the game, when it was apparent they'd lost, they reminded me of the humour, loyalty and passion of the City fans.

It was a hot day and as we increased our lead and the game

became a little easier, I was able to enjoy this last appearance for my club, knowing that my story couldn't have ended any better. It was a perfect day from the moment David gave us the lead. Gabriel Jesus showed us the full range of his skills, scoring two goals. Kevin came off the bench to play a big part in the second half, which was particularly deserved for him because of all his injury problems during the campaign. The final goals of this amazing treble season came from Raheem.

I suppose in the end people will say we won the final very comfortably, equalling the longstanding record for the biggest winning margin set by Bury in 1903. It seemed the perfect way to end my time at City. I could move on to the next phase of my life with my head held high.

Back in 1969 City had won the FA Cup wearing red and black striped shirts. Bernard Halford wore it in tribute when the club allowed him the chance to lift the cup along with the players in 2011, so I thought it was appropriate to do it again as I lifted the FA Cup in 2019 to honour Bernard and the City heroes of that previous era. It brought to an end the biggest part of my life as a professional footballer. During my ten years at City, I'd won the Premier League four times, the FA Cup twice, the League Cup four times and the Community Shield twice. The promises the club made to me and I made to them when I signed on 22 August 2008 had been kept and surpassed.

After we'd celebrated with our supporters on the Wembley pitch, the moment came to make one last speech as City captain, to my teammates and friends. It wasn't easy to keep control of my emotions, but here's what I said:

I just want to say thank you. Thank you for eleven years of experiences. Bad patches, good patches ... everything I have experienced with the club that I love. I'm so grateful. It's not going to be my best speech, because it's the most emotional one I have ever given in my life. I'm glad that this was my last game. I wouldn't have wanted it any different.

I just want to say that you guys are the best group of people I could have finished my City career with. I have gained new family members and I think you'll realise by the end, when you get to this point in your career, the people you remember are those who were there in special moments with you. Everyone here is now part of my family. The challenge for you boys is to be even better. It's difficult to say, when you have just won the English treble, but you haven't won the Champions League yet. That's your goal now.

You've got such a group of players that can achieve anything they want, don't ever let it slip. Before you know it, you will be doing a speech like me, crying, and then it's the end of it. Trust me, it goes that fast. So let's have a party, a good celebration and again, thank you very much.

EPILOGUE

During my time at City, I've come to understand something that's been at the club all the time. It's a certain attitude. In the beginning it was that if something could go wrong, it would, though that has changed now. But I've also come to understand that 'just get on with it' attitude. It's something that only Mancunians fully understand, but it suited me from day one. To get to where the club is today has been incredible and it's been unbelievable to be part of this journey. We needed to win that first FA Cup and to win the Premier League, but now we are ready for the Champions League. I don't think it was at the forefront of any City fan's dream when I arrived.

You can't look past the Aguero goal in 2012 as the single most significant event during my decade at City. That's the moment that defines so much for this club. A lot of the players coming through and playing in the current environment have to thank that squad, and Sergio in particular, for that goal. To me he's a hero, and I got to play with him every day. I see his flaws, but then I take a step back and realise how defining he has been and his goal has been for my career and for all City fans.

I remember the confusion we felt straight after he scored that goal, just like when I scored against United a few games earlier. It wasn't happiness or sadness or anything, it was simply confusion. What's happening? We'd never been in that position before, and we weren't sure then that we should be. When United were eight points ahead it seemed as though the league was done, and as a club it had felt like we'd given up when we lost to Arsenal away. Ultimately, we showed we had this team mentality and we came back and won it.

Since then we'd gone from strength to strength, and bringing in Pep as the manager was when we showed that we were only going to focus on the best, for he is the best in the business. And that's why his words about me after the parade around Manchester to celebrate our treble triumph meant so much to me: 'We are going to miss Vincent a lot. I think it was an incredible way to say goodbye. We are going to see each other in the future. He will come back, sooner or later. It's an incredible way to say goodbye with this incredible season, all together. He was a real captain. He helped us a lot.'

We've got used to going around Manchester on an end-of-season parade, although you never really get used to something like that. It's always great to see so many City fans proudly waving flags and cheering us. I knew when we arrived in the square there would be speeches, but I hadn't planned to drop the microphone at the end of my words to the crowd. I remember saying I was going to do it, as a laugh, before we went on the podium. Someone might have dared me to do it, but I can't remember who. At the end I just thought, *This is the way to go; if you're going to go, you've got to go properly.*

From the moment I scored the goal against Leicester, everything else felt like putting the finishing touches to my time at the club. Here's what I said to the crowd on the day of the parade:

> *I'll finish on this. You are the best club in the world. I don't care if you win the Champions League or not – you are the best club in the world, and remember it forever. These guys deserve all your love. Every day of the week, every single year, they work hard. This is the way I want to leave. I want to say thank you. I love you from my heart, I love you all. I'm out [drops microphone].*

I said so many goodbyes, but I've never been a player who dwells on what I've achieved. However, after the way my teammates reacted it gave me a reason to look back, to be grateful, to say my thank yous and lots of goodbyes. I don't think people can really imagine how grateful I am. I've given a lot, but I've received even more back. It's more than just the football; it's about the way I've been received in the city of Manchester. I've been able to feel at home and really believe that this is my city. I don't feel English, but I definitely feel Manc.

My final goodbye after my last season at Manchester City was this open letter to the fans:

> *Community Shield Winners!*
>   *Back 2 back League Cup Winners!*
>   *Back 2 back Champions of England!*
>   *FA Cup Winners!*

We've just seen the close of an incredible season. My eleventh as a Blue. I cannot believe I'm writing this but . . . my last as a Blue.

Countless times I've imagined this day, after all the end has felt nearby for so many years.

It still doesn't feel real. Man City has given me everything. I've tried to give back as much as I possibly could. How often does someone get the chance to end such an important chapter, representing a club with such great history and tradition in such a great fashion?

The time has come for me to go now.

As overwhelming as it is, I feel nothing but gratefulness. I am grateful to all those who have supported me on a special journey at a very special club.

I remember the first day as clear as I see the last. I remember the boundless kindness I have received from the people of Manchester.

I will never forget how all Manchester City fans remained loyal to me in good times and especially bad times. Against the odds you have always backed me and inspired me to never give up.

Sheikh Mansour changed my life and that of all the City fans around the world, for that I am forever grateful. A blue nation has risen and challenged the established order of things, I find that awesome.

I cherish the counsel and leadership of a good human being, Khaldoon Al Mubarak. Man City could not be in better hands.

A special word also to Pep and the backroom staff: you've been superb. You've followed me through so much hardship, but you made me come back stronger every time. Thank you so much.

I also want to express the love I have for my nearest and

dearest. It knows no boundaries. Carla, Sienna, Sire and Kai, the only quadruple that matters.

My Dad (Pierre), Christel and François, my true Invincibles. I live with only one regret. I would have loved to take my mother, Jocelyne, to the Etihad, seeing her chant the City songs next to my children and wife. I would have wanted her to see me happy, playing the game that I love at a club that I love. Deep down, I know she's been with us through all this time.

This is no goodbye, it's a see you later.

Love,

Vincent

I have a new challenge as player-manager at Anderlecht and the prospect of ever returning to City as manager in the future is the furthest thing from my mind right now, despite people suggesting the idea. I am like a player at the very beginning of his career. All I'm worried about is the next game. Once that's gone, my full attention moves on to the next game and so on. What will happen, will happen, but in the meantime I believe City have the right people in place and they're the same people I would have in those roles at the moment. They need to fully back those guys and that's the best thing for the club.

That said, I was flattered when Pep had the following to say about me, after the season was over, and maybe – having started this book with Kevin de Bruyne's thoughts – we should give him the last word:

One of the finest things about the season was his spirit. His shot, the desire to score a goal. When Vincent was fit he was important, he played an important role in our team, unfortunately sometimes that couldn't happen. This club is what it is because of the long history with the old players like Mike Summerbee, Colin Bell and other incredible people here.

Since Sheikh Mansour took over this club and Khaldoon was put in charge leading us, there are a few players that have changed this club. I'm thinking of Pablo Zabaleta, Joe Hart, Vincent Kompany, David Silva, Sergio Aguero — they are incredible players that have helped this club to make a step forward. I think Vincent leads these types of groups and he deserves all my respect.

The club I found when I arrived, he helped to build. With all the others we have tried to maintain it. It will be difficult to replace Vincent. Everyone is different, but he believes everything he says and everything he thinks. We will miss him. We will miss him a lot. I wish him all the best in the next step in his life, but he will always be an incredible part of the history of this club.